WHITE STAR PUBLISHERS

ITALY
from above

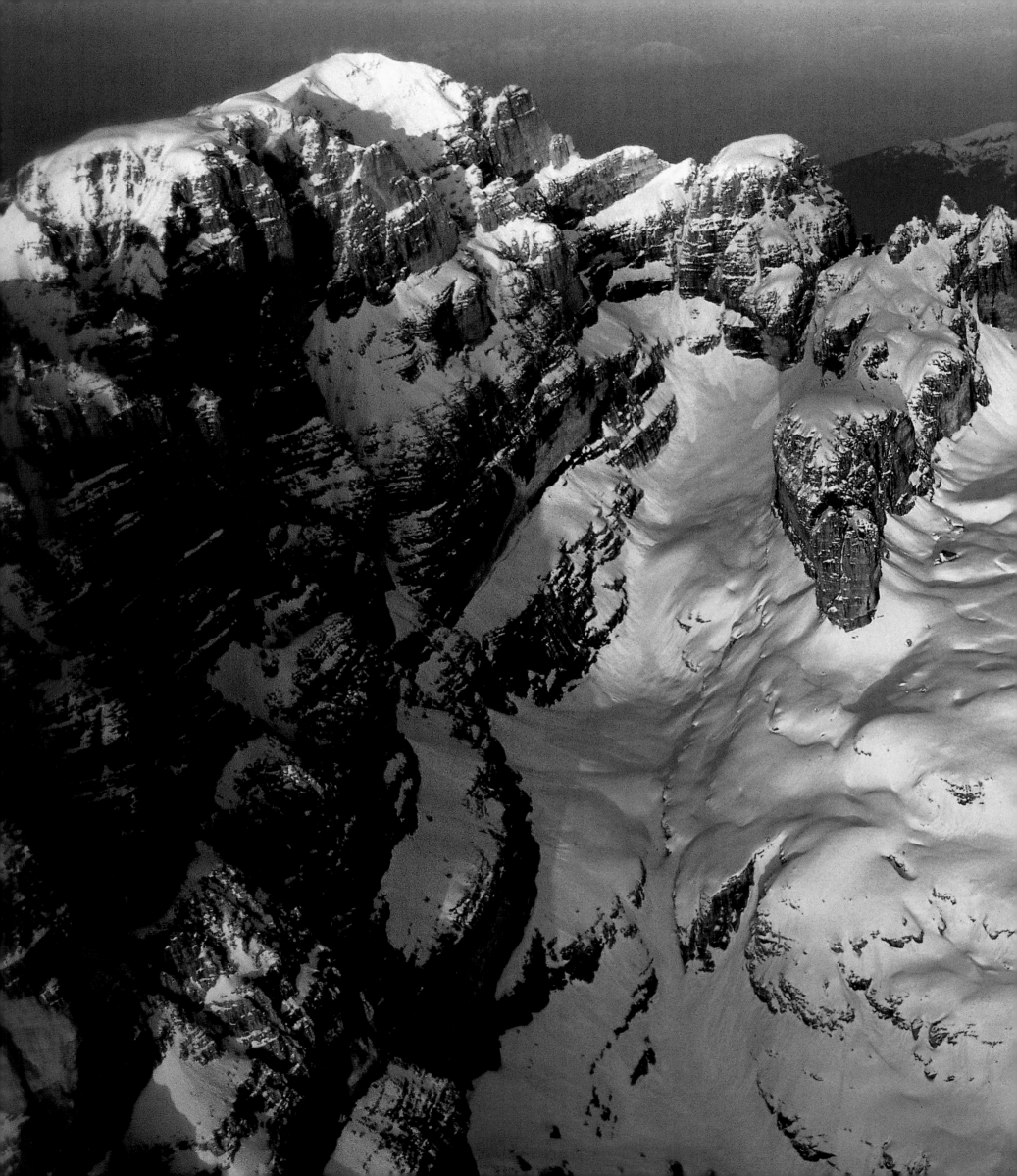

PHOTOGRAPHS
ANTONIO ATTINI
MARCELLO BERTINETTI

FOREWORD
FRANCO ZEFFIRELLI

INTRODUCTION
GIULIANO URBANI

TEXT
ALBERTO BERTOLAZZI

INCLUDED DVD "high above the Alps" FILMED BY CARLO DE FABIANIS

EDITORIAL DIRECTOR VALERIA MANFERTO DE FABIANIS   REDACTION MARIA VALERIA URBANI GRECCHI   GRAPHIC DESIGN CLARA ZANOTTI

BIOGRAPHIES

ANTONIO ATTINI

Antonio Attini was born in Turin in 1960 and has produced numerous reportages in Europe, Africa, Asia and America, published in the world's leading travel magazines. He has worked for Edizioni White Star since 1989, taking the photographs for numerous volumes belonging to the *Countries of the world*, *The world from the air* and *Places and History* series, and also participating in the production of various other prestigious works. He has been a member of the Kodak Gold Circle since 1994, with the standard of excellence. In recent years he has specialized in aerial photography, with reportages from the skies of America, Europe and Africa. His books include *Ireland from the air*, *America from the air*, *Chicago from the air*, *Hawaii from the air*, *New York from above*, *San Francisco from above* and *Ireland Flying High*, all published by White Star and already translated into ten languages.

MARCELLO BERTINETTI

Marcello Bertinetti was born in Vercelli in 1952. He became a national and international fencing champion and was a member of the Italian team at the 1976 Montreal Olympics. After obtaining a university degree in mechanical engineering, he started to take a keen interest in photography and became a freelance photographer in 1978. He has produced exclusive reportages for the world's most prestigious magazines, including *National Geographic*, *Geo*, *Newton - Japan*, *Paris Match*, *Figaro*, *Airone* and *Stern*.

He collaborates with the leading stock photography agencies, including Rapho, Photo Researchers, Focus and Pacific Press Service. He is the author of many successful photographic books, including *New York* (1982), published in various countries. He recently published *In the eye of Horus* and *Egypt, Flying High*, which has already been translated into 12 languages. In 1984 he founded the White Star publishing company with Valeria Manferto De Fabianis, flanking his profession as photographer with the job of publisher.

ALBERTO BERTOLAZZI

Alberto Bertolazzi was born in 1961 and studied philosophy at the University of Pavia. An attentive traveler and keen natural historian, after a brief period teaching, he started working for several newspapers, including *La Repubblica*, *La Stampa*, *Il Giornale Nuovo*, *Il Piccolo di Trieste* and *Il Giorno*, and periodicals, such as *Meridiani*, *Sestante* and *Panorama*. He was editor and subsequently editor-in-chief of the periodical *Notizia Oggi*. He has written *Lisbona* (1997), *Portugal* (1998) and *The Earth* (2004) for White Star Publishers and has worked on the texts of numerous other nature books.

CONTENTS

FRANCO ZEFFIRELLI

From the time he was a young child Leonardo used to climb to the summit of Montalbano, up to "his" rock that projected out over the Arno Valley beneath him. We know that it was his uncle Francesco, a young man, who used to guide him on these fantastic explorations, leading his youthful mind to contemplate the world from above, high up on that peak, which made him feel as if he were flying.

It was then that Leonardo began his fantastic relationship with creatures that have the gift and privilege of flight – imagining how they viewed the world on which he and other men were obliged to remain firmly anchored, merely able to walk upon it. This ardent desire to fly remained with Leonardo throughout his whole life; it motivated him to dedicate his most persistent research to the miracle of flight, studying and inventing machines and instruments that imitate the structures which Nature bestowed on birds.

Each time that I fly – and because of my profession I must do so often – I confess that I spend the entire time looking out of the window, contemplating the world that appears and disappears beneath the clouds, so varied and surprising, identical to those that Leonardo painted so often, imagining the world through a bird's-eye view.

This book – a truly splendid volume – awakens in me many astounding thoughts and fantasies; it also fuels my gratitude toward the progress that allows us not only to contemplate the most secret folds and recesses of the earth, but also reveals for us unknown, unexplored, and surprising realities – a gallery of the miracles of nature and humankind – bound together in a positive, extraordinary union.

To fly through the skies over Italy is a source of limitless wonder, almost a love affair. What else can match it? I am not speaking with the passion of a lover, but with that of an artist who finds himself in awe at the performance that the sky unveils for us, providing scenes of this extraordinary land that we suddenly seem to view as through the eye of God.

The accomplishment of including in one volume so many splendid images of Italy's ever-varied scenery, from such an original and dramatic viewpoint, in such an original form, deserves the gratitude reserved for a masterpiece.

Perhaps in viewing the rooftops and hidden gardens of Florence, the sand dunes of Sardinia, or Alpine peaks, revealed as visions of an unknown planet, we may measure, with a different perspective, the noble beauty of our motherland, and the gifts that we receive daily from its Creator.

Was this Leonardo's dream? To become a bird to better feel our humanity, to be more aware of the miraculous world around us?

Franco Zeffirelli

GIULIANO URBANI

I searched far and wide for a single word that would suffice to define this book. I needed a sort of epigraph that was as short as possible, which I obviously sought among the least trite adjectives for the description a work that is anything but trite and banal. However, at a certain point I had to give up, to avoid falling into one of the most stupid habits of recent years: that of using the wrong words, obviously inappropriate words, with the sole purpose of dazzling the reader, due to the wish to surprise or amaze at all costs, and in an invariably grotesque manner, to which we have unfortunately been accustomed.

Consequently, I fell back on an old, and probably slightly dated, term that nonetheless seemed to me to be the most appropriate for the purpose: edifying, a truly edifying book.

According to the dictionaries, edifying is something that instructs so as to encourage intellectual improvement. And so what better way of expressing our gratitude as readers for a volume such as this, which is capable of showing us new, unexpected and moving aspects of Italy? Moreover, *Italy, Emotions from the Air* is truly able to exert numerous edifying influences. First of all because it helps us to discover; in the sense that such a different viewpoint enables us to see hitherto unknown "faces" of reality, which we normally observe from radically different angles. These new visions thus represent unexpected new discoveries.

Furthermore, it helps us to extend, enrich and deepen our knowledge. I am thinking in particular of those incredible "models of cities" that appear from the aerial views of certain urban structures, with all their inestimable heritage of unique historical, political and aesthetic features.

26-27
Apulia – OSTUNI | A few kilometers from the Adriatic coast, between Monopoli and Brindisi, Ostuni's walls enclose an intricate white town, composed of Baroque palaces, flights of stairs, simple whitewashed houses and monumental Baroque churches.

28-29
Veneto – BURANO | The thriving island of Burano emerges from the center of the Venice Lagoon. Today the fishing village is renowned for its lace production and the multicolored houses that overlook its canals.

Finally, they help us to love and thus also better protect and conserve (as recalled in the introduction to the book) the treasures of our inimitable country.

The overall picture is a highly illuminating cross-section of Italy as a "whole". Nature and culture as parts of a single great human story. Monuments and landscapes, cities and countryside and towns and villages become the tesserae of an extraordinary mosaic that also constitutes a sort of display case of our civilizations, past and present. In this sense, viewing everything from above – as this splendid book enables us to do – truly helps to enrich our knowledge. Above all, with the purpose of protecting and valorizing Italy as a "whole", by the creation of legal institutions that do not dismember it into many isolated compartments, but instead envisage it as a sort of "integrated system", where nature and culture, landscape and art are always seen as completely interdependent aspects.

When Italy finally adopted the first Code for Heritage and Landscape of its long history last year, the Prince of Wales asked me why it hadn't been drawn up sooner, in view of the nation's very particular origins. I had no trouble answering him that, unfortunately, in this respect we had no foreign model on which to base it, considering the unique and unrepeatable nature of the Italian experience. However, leaving aside my highly predictable answer, the question was entirely legitimate.

It is true: with all the wonders that we possess, we should have thought of it decades ago, thus avoiding a great deal of the defacement of our landscape, towns and monuments with which we are all sadly familiar.

Giuliano Urbani

Giuliano Urbani

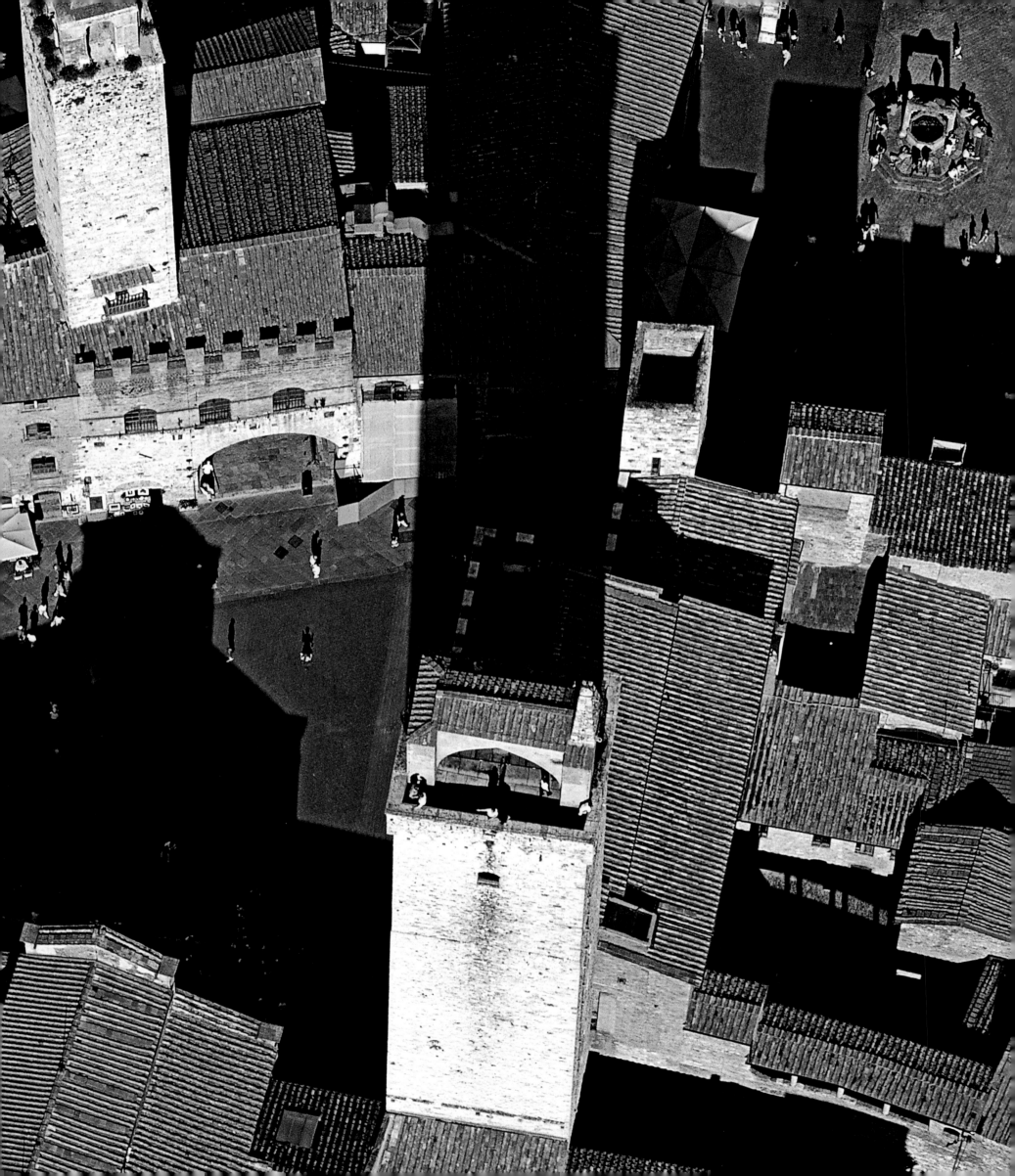

THE ENCHANTED PENINSULA

ITALIAN SKIES

Three elements must exist for the production of a far-ranging pictorial record such as this volume. The first is a passion for flying, which talented photographers must be able to combine with a spectacular visionary capacity. Next, a sense of admiration for Italy's priceless riches and the conviction that the nation's artistic, historical and natural heritage is so scattered that its true extent cannot easily be recognized – as if the country itself were partly veiled by its sheer vastness. Lastly, there must be the determination – shared by all who are truly entranced by beauty – to contribute to the appreciation and protection of the treasures of the Italian peninsula and islands. These three forces must be harnessed to support a single aim: to reconstruct the great Italian mosaic by means of aerial photographs, offering the reader a single, marvelous picture.

A passion for flying involves the rediscovery of the sky above Italy. This unusually blue expanse is clear on winter days, damp and foggy in fall, slightly veiled by heat in summer and furrowed by light, fast-moving rain clouds in spring. This sky has a thousand scents grassy Alpine meadows awaking from hibernation, the sunflowers and poppies of the Tuscan hills, the factory smoke and visible antiquity of the large cities and the salt and rosemary of the coasts – and has inspired the genius of architects and dreamers and guided great navigators during the long starry nights.

The creatures that inhabit the Italian sky are highly privileged: they glide silently above boundless Mediterranean vistas, circle woodlands, dive headfirst along dizzy mountain cliffs and slowly and composedly fly over the roofs and piazzas of a thousand cities. They experience the magic of flight, which reveals hidden views of the most evocative corners and exposes the utter beauty – stripped of mystery of a country with multiple identities and fabulous delights. This explains why aer-

34-35
Sardinia – COSTA SMERALDA

The crescent white sand beach of Lu Portu de li Coggi, near Porto Romazzino epitomizes the charm of the entire Costa Smeralda, which is studded with small coral sand beaches enclosed by wind-beaten rocks.

36-37
Piedmont – VERCELLI AREA

The Po River Valley is an extensive, fertile and easily irrigable plain, where the hand of man has created enchanted landscapes. The "patchwork sea" of regularly divided paddy fields is flooded in the spring and irregularly reflects the light of sunset, like a shattered mirror.

ial photographs exert an incredible attraction: they offer us the wings for which we have always yearned and let us fly free beyond the usual viewpoint, high among the clouds. Up where the air starts to thin, a new world of wide open spaces, grazing light and completely unexpected colors unfolds before the astonished eyes of the photographer, in a series of moving views that slip rapidly away, uniting the essence of entire territories in a single embrace. The second element entails a tour of the country's greater- and lesser-known treasures and the intriguing revelation that art and nature, history and environment are intimately linked in a special way in Italy. This is a land of great scenic wealth, spectacular coasts, lofty mountains, intriguing hills, unique cities and monuments and also a land of great geniuses, for Italy has cultivated beauty, art and science for many centuries. The love of natural harmony and the magnificence of the works of man have been refined by hundreds of years of history and cultural admixtures of all kinds, giving modern Italy an extraordinary and unrivaled heritage. The grand tours of 17th-century foreign visitors were often a tribute to the solemn majesty of artistic mon-

uments. Overwhelmed by the sheer power of immediately engaging masterpieces and exhausted by direct contact with such great beauty, they would fall to the ground, overwhelmed by the sight of them, succumbing to Stendhal's syndrome a splendid linguistic invention capable of summing up the disorienting effect of the sublime.

Is there a relationship between the natural wealth and the artistic production of a country? Would the Mona Lisa have been painted with soft and sinuous features and against a backdrop of hills if Leonardo da Vinci had not grown up in the Tuscan countryside? Would Brunelleschi have conceived the astounding geometrical structure of the dome of Santa Maria del Fiore if he had not been acquainted with the harmonious landscapes around Florence? And do the Venetian palaces not owe part of their sweet lightness to the magical reflections of the waters that lap against them? Art, like history, is not detached from the location in which it is expressed. Italy, by a gift of fate, is one of the few countries in the world whose environmental and cultural heritages shine without one submerging the other. Consequently a journey through the Ital-

The grazing light in this winter picture heightens the grandeur of the Alpine peaks of the Valle d'Aosta. The bulk of Mont Blanc rises up unchallenged in the background on the left, while the outline of the Grand Combin can be discerned in the center.

ian microcosm is an uninterrupted alternation of emotions, stimulated not only by the turquoise reflections of the Sardinian waters and the majesty of the Dolomites, but also by the ruins of mysterious Pompeii or a stroll through the walled city of Siena; on the hills and glaciers, coral sands and fabulous islands as well as the masterpieces of architecture and the still-warm traces left by legendary figures of antiquity, the magic of the purest art. However, like a museum that is too large to be visited in a single day, Italy offers its wealth so generously that it confuses the untrained eye. Our distracted attention as land travelers frequently prevents us from sensing the complexity of beauty, for we are used to seeing the fragments of places that we visit pass before our eyes like the frames of a film that unfolds too fast, not allowing us to grasp the plot. The third of the elements underlying *Italy, Emotions from the Air* stems from our fear of losing a part of what we hold dear. During our journey above the peninsula, our privileged vantage point enabled us to realize how the most beautiful flowers are in danger of withering, due to carelessness or mere disinterest. Consequently, we decided to transform the aerial photographs into a book and tribute, capable of arousing joy, respect and love of beauty within the reader. The book is not an accusation, but rather a catalogue of light, color and form awaiting to be admired, with the purpose of reminding us that one day all of this could disappear, erased by our own amnesia.

Two men bewitched by the charm of their unique country and enamored of the Italian sky made this extremely ambitious project possible: Marcello Bertinetti and Antonio Attini, who took the photographs for this book, accepting a grueling but fruitful task never before carried out in such a comprehensive manner. Indeed, they spent over 270 hours aboard small aircraft, helicopters and hot-air balloons flying the length and breadth of Italy, from Lampedusa to the peaks of the Dolomites, from Sardinia to the Adriatic coast and from the great cities to the archaeological sites. The result is a collection of thousands of photographs representing each of the legs of this fantastic itinerary above the land of wonders. Great dedication has been lavished on this volume's splendid panoramic pictures; they seek to evoke in the viewer the same sudden excitement that strikes the aerial observer faced with spectacles of rare beauty.

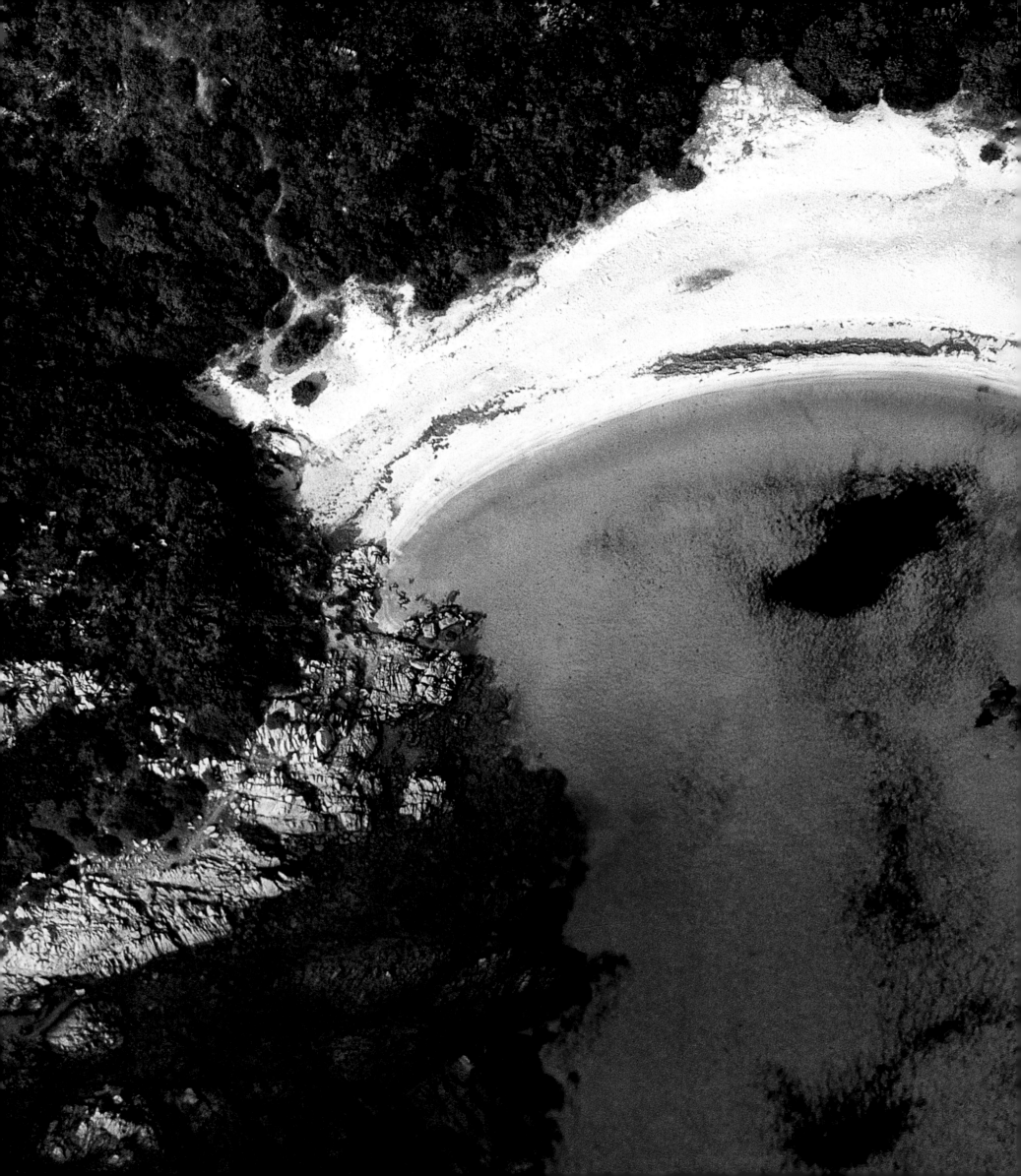

PEARL OF THE MEDITERRANEAN

The sea as a limit and as a treasure.

The sea that distances and unites.

The sea as an inheritance and as a chain.

Italy is a great ship floating on the

Mediterranean, which owes the most

important chapters of its history to the sea.

PEARL OF THE MEDITERRANEAN

LANDS IN THE BLUE

41 | Rocks clawed by the
Sardinia – COSTA SMERALDA | wind and waves stretch
out into the sea.

A boot kicking out into the Mediterranean Sea, or – according to others – an enormous floating raft with an uneven outline, whose borders have been eroded by the incessant action of the waves, Italy has almost 5,600 miles of coastline including Sicily and Sardinia, which alone account for half the total length. A long chain stretching from the Gulf of Lion to Dalmatia, creating bays and inlets, promontories and beaches, cliffs and rocks, overlooking a palette of ever-changing cobalt and turquoise. The coasts are rocky, wedged between high mountains and deep seas, as in much of Liguria; or they have long shores with wide beaches, like those bordering the Adriatic Sea, formed by thousands of years of river deposits and constituting the natural continuation of gently sloping hills. It is the magic of a country –Italy –which has had to come to terms with the sea since ancient times, obtaining sustenance from it and sometimes riches, joys and sorrows. Extraordinary cities have flourished along these coasts, even though the greatest of all, Rome, was never a true maritime power, unlike the republics of Genoa, Venice, Pisa and Amalfi. At the height of their splendor these city-states acquired fabulous riches from the Mediterranean, which are still reflected in their artistic heritages. Adventurous men and pioneers, from Christopher Columbus to Giuseppe Garibaldi, took to the sea from Italy's coast, while the ships of occupying and liberating forces anchored off its shores. Today the same coves that witnessed the landings of the Phoenicians, Greeks, Normans and the World War II Allies are frequented by pleasure boaters, who consider the Italian waters to be a sort of quintessential paradise. We are aboard a glider. Flying without engine power, we soar with the eyes and wings of a seagull, along the line where the waves break, on the border between land and sea. Beneath us, the realm of olive trees and flowers gives way to high, rocky coasts, inlets and promontories: this is the Liguria of Portofino and Porto Venere –green rocky fingers that stretch out and disappear into the deep, almost black, blue sea, without any reflections. The small houses appear like cherries on a great cake, while the sails and fishing boats leave foamy white trails. The Ligurian Sea has no transparent effects, rather it resembles ink, which becomes watercolor toward the rocks. It is completely different from the Argentario Peninsula and the numerous rocks that form the prelude to the Tuscan Archipelago, with its tortuous coastline marked with bays and indentations and mitigated by splendid sandy beaches. The Uccellina National Park sums up this part of the Italian coast in a picture-postcard view, for it is a great patch of maritime pines, crossed by rivers that flow into the sea, forming colored effects as they mingle with the currents, fringed by a long fine sandy beach, and surrounded by high green mountains and dark pools.

When viewed from the air, each Italian island resembles a jewel fallen from Venus' necklace, although this mythological description actually applies properly only to the Tuscan Archipelago. Indeed, this fantastic necklace was a gift of Paris, but slipped out of Venus' hands into the sea opposite the Argentario Peninsula. The jewels formed the islands of Gorgona, Capraia, Pianosa, Elba, Montecristo, Giannutri and Giglio. Elba is the largest and has a vaguely triangular shape. In the areas that are not covered by vegetation or marked by houses and roads, the naked bedrock has unusual iridescent glints, which has conditioned its history. Indeed, they reveal the island's ore deposits, which have colored it shades of emerald green, ocher and brown, with matt or shiny effects, and made it a sought-after quarry for many centuries. Today the mining has practically ceased, but the colors remain. The dominant shade of the island is nonetheless green: the hillsides are covered with vineyards, which have replaced the thick forests of antiquity, felled to fuel the furnaces. Surrounding the island are the stunning turquoise waters, like the splendid Tyrrhenian Sea that laps the sandy beaches. Capraia is nature, not in the pure state like Montecristo, which has been a nature reserve since 1971, or Gorgona, with its thick pine and olive groves and holm-oak woods, but very scenic, evocative and powerfully emotional. Its inland area is covered with low maquis, which forms an unbroken carpet and an impenetrable tangle when viewed from the air. Its turquoise waters are fringed by cliffs and little coves, rising above their reflections like multicolored and conceited peacocks. Sardinia, just a few miles away, seems to have been modeled by the wind and waves, which have scourged, cut and stripped the rock of the northeastern part of the island, carving the coast into a thousand coves and smashing it into a myriad of fragments, which form the Maddalena Archipelago. The action of the currents and tides has pulverized rock, coral and shells to form the typical white sand, creating splendid Caribbean scenes in the heart of the Mediterranean. The Maddalena Archipelago has the most Caribbean appearance of the numerous Sardinian islands: from Maddalena Island, the only permanently inhabited one of the group, to Budelli, whose pink beach is one of the most beautiful in the world, the archipelago is made up of granite fragments smoothed and unpredictably shaped by the wind and sandy coves, which interrupt the perilous rock-studded coasts. Viewed from above, they look like crumbs of red land, the largest of which are covered with thick pinewoods and colorful perfumed maquis. The wind has also modeled the islands of the Sulcis Archipelago, where its erosive action on the main island of San Pietro is clearly visible from the sky. Its grottoes and inlets evocatively open onto permanently choppy sea, revealing the bare rock and the numerous colored minerals that compose it. Wild landscapes are visible from the sky, with turquoise pools and inlets resembling little fjords. Cala Domesticus is a claw mark inflicted on the land by the sea, only slightly soothed by a crescent beach of fine sand, while unknown islets bear names that originated in the imagination of sailors such as Pan di Zucchero. To the east, along the Pontine Plain, the coastal dunes covered with maquis, lakes and forests of oak, ash, elm and eucalyptus slip beneath our wings. Beyond Mount Circeo, the coast is enclosed by the highlands that announce the Campanian Apennines, forcing it into the gulfs of Gaeta, Naples and Salerno. Offshore we can see the Pontine Islands, Ischia, Procida and Capri. The *piscinae* of Ponza, the largest and most famous of the Pontine Islands, are clearly visible from the glider: in Roman times the fish that reached the tables of the capital city –perhaps in the form of *garum*–was farmed here. Ponza, like Ventotene and Santo Stefano, is a prelude to the Campanian Islands. Ischia is a volcanic island, like Procida and Vivara. It is large and luxuriant, and an aerial tour reveals its extensive citrus groves, elegant vineyards and a large castle dominating an islet. Ischia, Procida (showing the outline of the craters that form its sinuous coastline) and Vivara close the Gulf of Naples to the northwest. The land covering the rock of the Amalfi coast is prone to landslides and has thus been almost completely terraced, with orange, lemon, fig and almond trees, vegetables, flowers and vines, which jostle for space with the increasingly rare Mediterranean bushes. The uninterrupted succession of houses and towns forms a unique patchwork with the terraced farmland. The stepped land creates unexpected effects of light and shade, especially towards sunset, when the terraces fall away towards the coast, creating green and yellow waves on the mountainsides that resemble the sea.

Our flight continues along cliffs and promontories and across gulfs of rare beauty, until reaching Calabria, whose Tyrrhenian coastline has a few short stretches of low, sandy shore. The turbulent currents around the Strait of Messina color the wind-rippled waters every shade of blue. This is the realm of Scylla and Charybdis, capricious deities that control the destiny of sailors. It is the meeting point of two seas and only the high mountainous land that forms the Calabrian backbone seems to be able to resist the impact of the moving masses of water.

Throughout the world, and in Italy in particular, islands are controversial places rich in symbols and meanings often unrelated to their morphological structure. The Mediterranean island is a microcosm where men and gods meet. Greek mythology was inherited and largely adopted by the Romans and subsequently all the Italian peninsula's peoples associated islands with the concepts of peace and asceticism: peace because of the islands' isolation from common troubles and asceticism because few people know how to

enjoy their precious treasures and harvest their bitter and well-defended fruits. From this point of view Sicily, like Sardinia, is more of a continent than an island, owing to a series of historical, anthropological and administrative reasons. The African coast clearly reveals the history of the Mediterranean and the entire terrestrial crust. Underwater paradises summing up the biological and scenic wealth of a transitory world, stretching from the Red Sea to the Atlantic, extend to reach nearby and distant archipelagoes: the Eolian Islands and Ustica to the north, the Egadi Islands to the west and Pantelleria and the Pelagian Islands to the south. Stromboli is the easternmost of the Eolian Islands and a permanently active volcano. Not far away, the islet of Strombolicchio rises out of the sea like the nose of a curious dolphin, while the other islands of the archipelago are visible from the opposite side of Stromboli: Basiluzzo, entirely composed of lava, Panarea, Salina, Lipari and Vulcano, which has long been a popular holiday destination. Farther west are the more secluded islands of Filicudi and Alicudi where the deep greens of the olive trees, the lively shades of the flowering caper bushes and the yellows and reds of the reeds and prickly pears. From Ustica, a natural marine park and diver's paradise, our flight takes us straight to the Egadi Islands. The yellow tuff islands of Levanzo and Favignana and multicolored Marettimo are set in the sea off Trapani. However, they are not the southernmost frontier of Italy, because much farther off, beyond the mountainous, green and unspoiled island of Marettimo, it is possible to glimpse Pantelleria, the fourth-largest Italian island. This volcanic land is heralded by the gray jets of steam that it throws up toward the sky. It is an island of raw colors, lunar landscapes and rugged coasts. In those areas unable to resist the erosive action of wind and wave, wounded, carved and battered rocks seem to retreat from the sea, bent by the brutality of the elements. The Pelagian Islands are the most remote Italian scraps of land. Linosa, black like Pantelleria, and limestone Lampedusa, rolling but in some places inaccessible, are far more African than European in character. Only one group of Italian islands escapes the embrace of the Tyrrhenian Sea: the Tremiti Islands. These are rugged islands, despite the gentle sandy appearance of their coasts. Caprara is uninhabited, San Nicola is barren and only San Domino has a large pine grove and wide expanses of maquis. All are visibly unspoiled, with dazzling white beaches, cliffs, grottoes and cobalt-blue sea. Apart from the Southern Basin, where depths can reach almost 3,300 feet, the Adriatic Sea resembles a great, slightly submerged terrace north of the dreamy Gargano Peninsula. Its color-light blue near the coast and greenish farther off – betrays the sandy nature of the seafloor. The profile of the coastline is also flat, apart from rare coastal lakes and even more infrequent mountainous promontories. However, marshes and lagoons, islets and reed thickets announce the Po Delta. The mingling waters of this magical microcosm make the water brackish, while the air is permeated by the scent of seaweed mixed with stagnant river air. The Venice, Marano and Grado lagoons are a fabulous world, opaque like an uncut diamond waiting for its full splendor to be revealed. The coastline becomes lower after the Gulf of Venice, furrowed by the rivers that flow parallel to the sea. Here the rugged rocky coast with lush vegetation is similar to that of Istria and Dalmatia. The presence of seabirds used to warn sailors of their proximity to the coast, although to us lovers of beauty the flight of seagulls acts as a reminder of the existence of a marvelous means of traveling over expanses of water to reach scraps of distant land: gliding through the sky, riding the wind, free to change course and altitude at will, dominating the horizon and letting the rippled surface below slip past. Our photographic journey around the splendid Italian coast takes advantage of this lightness. Our course will take us from west to east, heading south across the Tyrrhenian Sea and the magnificent clusters of Tuscan, Sardinian, Campanian and Sicilian islands, before turning northward again, seeking the other end of this never-ending thread stretching between Ventimiglia and Trieste, with its unique beauty and infinite ability to astonish.

48-49 | The evocative village of San Rocco is perched high on the Portofino promontory, overlooking the Gulf of Tigullio. The outskirts and port of
Liguria – RIVIERA DI LEVANTE | Genoa can be glimpsed in the distance, fading into the fog.

50
Liguria – RIVIERA DI LEVANTE
Portofino is a splendid crescent that has remained unspoiled over the centuries. The promontory, which culminates in Punta Chiappa and Punta Portofino, is a nature reserve: a paradise of chestnut trees and maritime pines, dotted with marvelous period villas. Elegant Art Nouveau style houses accessed by narrow carriage roads are set in the lush vegetation, while steep paths lead down the mountainside to the sea.

51
Liguria – RIVIERA DI LEVANTE
The enchanting inlet of San Fruttuoso is closed by the rocky headland of the Torretta, which culminates (above left) in Mount Portofino. The Bay of Capodimonte can be made out on the right, with the abbey in the background.

52-53
Liguria – RIVIERA DI LEVANTE
The Cinque Terre occupy an enchanting stretch of coast surrounded by spectacular terraced hills. This view shows the village of Manarola, dominated by a sea of renowned vineyards.

54 top
Tuscany – PIANOSA | The flat limestone island of Pianosa is the fifth largest of the Tuscan Archipelago and is practically uninhabited. The old jail, from which roads depart to each corner of the island, can be seen in the photograph.

54 bottom
Tuscany – ELBA | With its transparent sea and rocky coasts, interrupted by a few small coves, Elba is perhaps the brightest of the seven pearls that constitute the Tuscan Archipelago. Small villages, such as Marina di Campo (left), microscopic beaches, like Straccoligno (right), and sheer cliffs make it a dreamy seaside paradise.

55
Tuscany – ELBA | This kind of watercolor rainbow is formed by Elba's sea, sand and vegetation, making it resemble a deserted crescent moon waiting to be conquered.

Ventotene is a long curl of land floating on the lower Tyrrhenian Sea. From above it is characterized by the concrete and rock crescent of the new port that, with Punta Eolo (right), closes the northern part of the island.

56 bottom

Lazio – PONTINE ISLANDS The little island of Santo Stefano, a block of granite with little vegetation and no natural landing places, rises out of the sea a few miles from Ventotene, whose outline can be made out in the upper part of the pictures.

57

Lazio – PONTINE ISLANDS Santo Stefano is home to an old Bourbon jail. The semicircular 17th-century fortification was built to imprison convicts serving life sentences.

58 | The volcanic rocks have been shaped into coves and cliffs, grottoes and headlands, like the
Lazio – PONTINE ISLANDS | famous and evocative Capo Bianco.

59 | Ponza's volcanic coasts, devoured by the power of the waves, offer an infinite array of forms and dazzling colors.
Lazio – PONTINE ISLANDS | The island is a constantly alternating series of small bays, such as that enclosing the town of Ponza (opposite, lower left) or Cala dell'Acqua (opposite, lower right), and rocky promontories, like Punta Madonna (opposite, lower center) that is the resting place of a small cemetery.

Clinging to the rocks of the headland from which it takes its name, the Punta della Guardia Lighthouse seems to hide behind a veil of clouds.

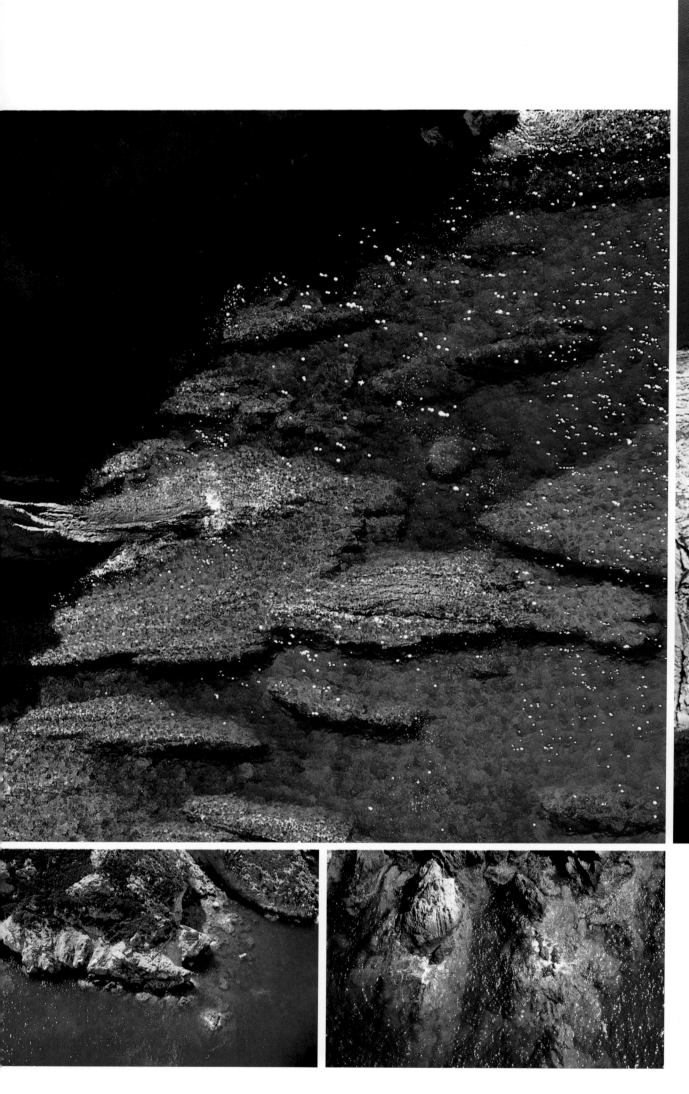

62 top
Lazio – PONTINE ISLANDS | Turquoise glints heighten the beauty of the sea that laps the island of Zannone, a small scrap of land covered with dense maquis that covers an area barely larger than half a square mile.

62 bottom and 62-63
Lazio – PONTINE ISLANDS | Palmarola, Ponza's historical appendage, is made up of rocks, grottoes and cliffs. The ancient inhabitants of the archipelago carved unique cave-houses out of the white rock faces that overlook its waters. The island is of volcanic origin and still displays the signs of ancient explosions and fractures, like the arch of vitrified lava between Punta Mezzogiorno and Punta Vardella.

64 | The little town of Capri is a precious pearl that forms a gentle curve along the high ground that occupies the central
Campania – CAPRI | part of the island. The passage of the millennia has only served to heighten the magical atmosphere of this thoroughly Mediterranean sanctuary.

65 | Capri offers incomparable views, which also bewitched the ancient world. The island has always had a special
Campania – CAPRI | charm, associated with its high rocky coasts and splendid Faraglioni cliffs (above) that overlook the sapphire sea.

66-67 | Vegetation-covered cliffs plunge sheer to the
Campania – SORRENTO PENINSULA | sea and the white rock and Mediterranean scrub are reflected in the dark waters of the coast, creating a dreamlike landscape.

Artificial terraces and natural steps mingle with the Amalfi highlands to create a unique stratification, partially hidden by the thick vegetation. Some of the houses of Ravello, one of the pearls of this stretch of coast, can be seen on the left.

70 | The hills of the Sorrento Peninsula alternate with deep, wide valleys, majestic mountains and flights of
Campania – SORRENTO PENINSULA | steps formed by terraces sloping down towards the sea. These are occupied by olive, orange and lemon groves, vineyards, aristocratic villas and country houses.

71 | The Amalfi Coast is delineated by a succession of inlets, and delightful little villages overlook the Gulf of
Campania – AMALFI COAST | Salerno: Atrani (visible in the foreground), then Minori and Maiori, while Scala and Ravello can be glimpsed clinging to the slopes.

72-73 | Positano, Amalfi, Atrani, Ravello, Maiori, Minori: centuries of terracing were required to enable the construction
Campania – AMALFI COAST | of stable settlements on the mountainsides. The result, viewed from above, is a spectacular picture of overlapping waves, which slope down towards the sea.

74 | The bare northeastern coast of Sardinia is a dream for sea lovers, with its many gorges and sandy
Sardinia – COSTA SMERALDA | coves lapped by clear, clean waters.

75 | Several of the crescent beaches have a tropical air, such as the legendary Pink Beach of Budelli
Sardinia – MADDALENA ARCHIPELAGO | (opposite): a gleaming gateway to a lost paradise. The pink hue for which it is famed derives from the
eroding of the red corals that thrive nearby.

76-77 | The west coast slope gently towards the sea behind Arbatax. The continuous erosion of the waves does not spare even
Sardinia – COSTA REI | the granite rocks, which the force of the wind and water has carved into bays such as the one shown here. In the center of
the photograph, a bed of seaweed plays on the viewer's imagination, suggesting the outline of a giant ray.

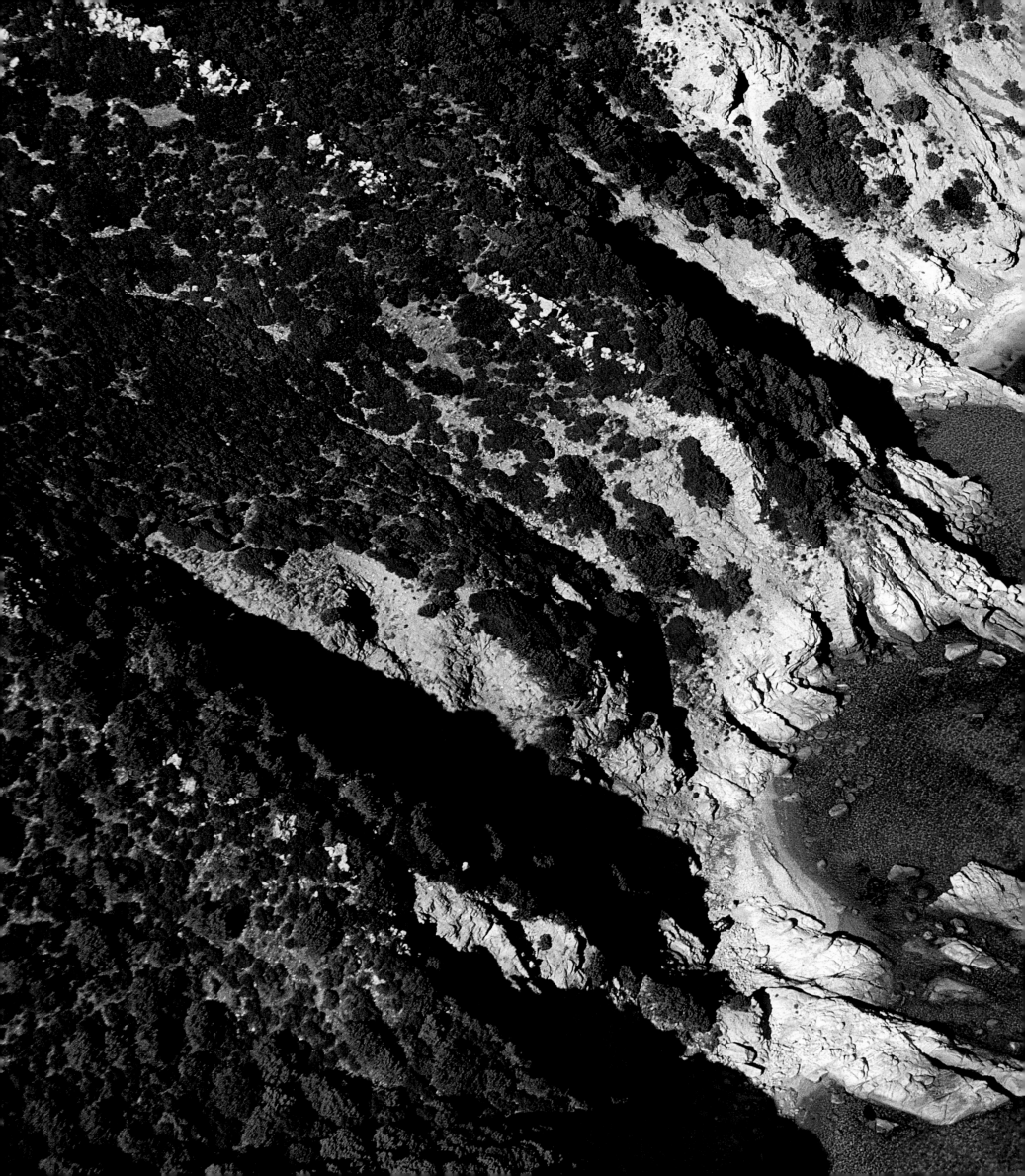

78 | A winding road leads from Alghero to Capo Caccia, the westernmost point of Sardinia. Its squiggly
Sardinia – NURRA | course cuts through vegetation that resembles a thin green film resting on the massive promontory
that drops sheer to the sea from dizzy heights.

79 | Capo Testa rises opposite Corsica, where its huge smooth and iridescent gray-pink granite rocks
Sardinia – GALLURA | plunge into one of the most beautiful stretches of sea in the world: the Strait of Bonifacio.

80 and 81 | Splendid beaches of fine white sand are lapped by the gentle waters of Stintino, and sandy islets
Sardinia – NURRA | dissolve in the turquoise and azure depths. Just off the coast, fishermen draw strange geometric
patterns with their nets.

82-83 | The southwestern coast of Sardinia offers lunar landscapes where the combination of sand, vegetation and saltwater
Sardinia – IGLESIENTE | create abstract patterns, such as that shown here, formed by the tides on the coast north of Buggerru, near Piscinas.

84
Sardinia — IGLESIENTE

Granite headlands and seaweed-covered sandbanks create evocative forms along the western coast of Sardinia.

84-85
Sardinia – IGLESIENTE | The ancient Spanish tower still stands guard at the entrance to Cala Domestica, a fjord-like inlet of water wedged between the ocher rocks on this stretch of coast, enclosed by low dunes of fine sand.

86-87
Sardinia – IGLESIENTE | Enchanted islets emerge from the cobalt-blue sea along the shores of the island. This one is known as Pan di Zucchero and is a fragment of coast eroded by the waves that stands a few miles off the island of San Pietro.

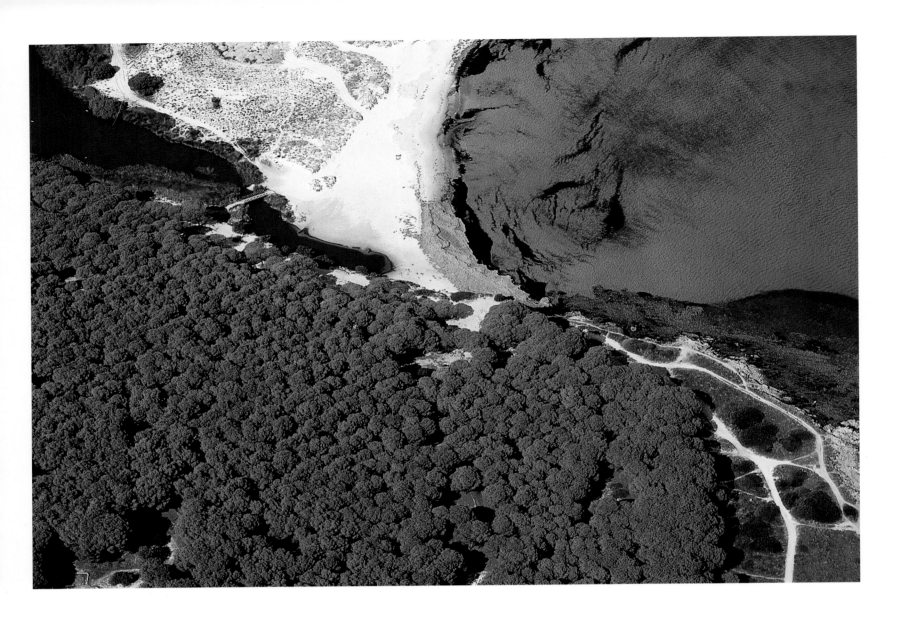

88 | A forest of maritime pine stretches down to the sapphire blue sea. A triangle of white beach is wedged
Sardinia — SOUTHERN COAST | between the sea and the vegetation, creating this unique geometric composition.

89 | A lucky bather has anchored his boat to enjoy the calm and crystal-clear sea off Capo Passero.
Sicily — SOUTHERN COAST | The extraordinary transparency of these deep waters creates an illusion of shallowness from above.

90-91
Sicily – EOLIAN ISLANDS | Vulcano, like Stromboli, is an island of fire. Around the Great Crater – one of the two currently active cones – are the "fumaroles", an expanse of sulfurous vapors, which tinge the island yellow and ocher.

90
Sicily – EOLIAN ISLANDS | The ancient whitewashed stone houses of Salina have been converted for use by tourists and form a white blot amid the maquis.

92-93 | A plume of steam rises skyward from the gaping mouth of Stromboli's volcano. Far away, beyond the green slopes
Sicily – EOLIAN ISLANDS | and white houses that cling to them, lies the turquoise expanse of the lower Tyrrhenian Sea.

94-95 | Terraced olive groves, small splashes of caper bushes and a few yellow tuff houses slope
Sicily – EOLIAN ISLANDS | gently towards the sea on Alicudi, the most westerly of the Eolian Islands.

96-97 | Crumbs of Sicily float off its western
Sicily – EGADI ISLANDS | coast: these are the Egadi Islands, a
paradise of sun and sand. Favignana,
in this photo, is flat and scorched, but
lapped by clear, warm waters.

97 | This ancient *tonnara* (tuna fishery), which
Sicily – SOUTHERN COAST | stands on a small scrap of land on the
southern coast of Sicily, is lapped by the
food-rich currents in which the fish are
caught.

Isola dei Conigli rises out of the sea opposite the southern coast of Lampedusa, the most distant of the Pelagie Islands from the Sicilian coast. This bare, rugged island conceals precious underwater treasures, making it a diver's paradise.

99 top, bottom center and right
Sicily – PELAGIE ISLANDS

It is possible to obtain a clear picture of Lampedusa's character by flying over the island: the limestone platform is inaccessible from the north and lower and eroded to the southeast, where the Capo Grecale Lighthouse stands.

99 bottom left
Sicily – PELAGIE ISLANDS

The Spiaggia dei Conigli, one of the last Italian nesting sites of the loggerhead turtle, is in one of the most evocative spots of Lampedusa.

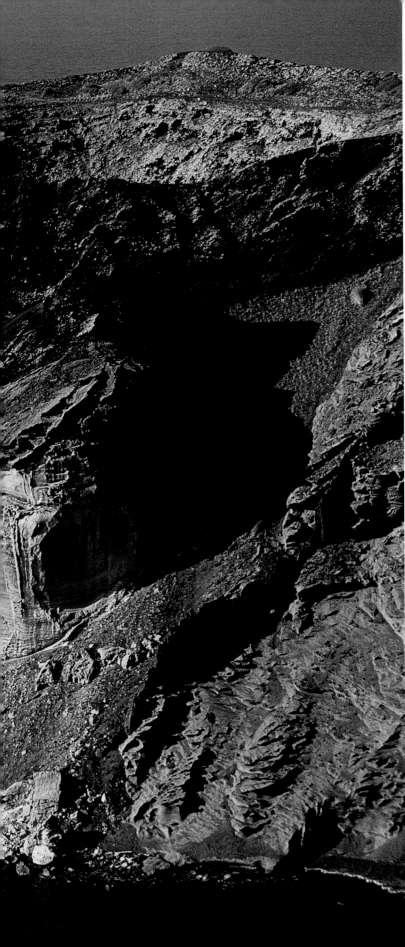

100-101
Sicily – PELAGIE ISLANDS | Linosa is an island of dazzling colors and clear contrasts: the minerals deposited during volcanic eruptions, such as the yellow sulfur of Cala Pozzolana di Ponente, create a palette that also includes the green of the sparse vegetation and the white of the houses.

101
Sicily – PELAGIE ISLANDS | Modeled by the waves, the black, jagged rocks that reach out towards the African coast recall Pantelleria's volcanic origins.

102 | Apulia – SALENTO | At Santa Maria di Leuca, the Ionian Sea merges with the Adriatic and the West with the East. The two seas meet beyond the headland of Santa Maria, watched over by the tall white lighthouse.

103 | Apulia – GARGANO | Between Mattinata and Vieste, the coast of the Gargano Peninsula forms a series of coves and inlets, carved out of white rocks veined with chert, between rocky peaks that tower above sandy shores lapped by the sea. The photograph shows the Faraglione di Pizzomunno, the Gargano's highest cliff.

104-105 and 105 top
Apulia – TREMITI ISLANDS

The island of Caprara is a knotty apostrophe set in the sea off the Gargano Peninsula, at the very heart of Adriatic Sea. An ancient lighthouse with flashing lantern stands on a projection of the narrow Punta Secca Peninsula.

105 bottom
Apulia – TREMITI ISLANDS

Punta Diamante is the northernmost tip of San Domino, the largest of the Tremiti Islands. The small island of Cretaccio can be discerned to the northeast and San Nicola further east.

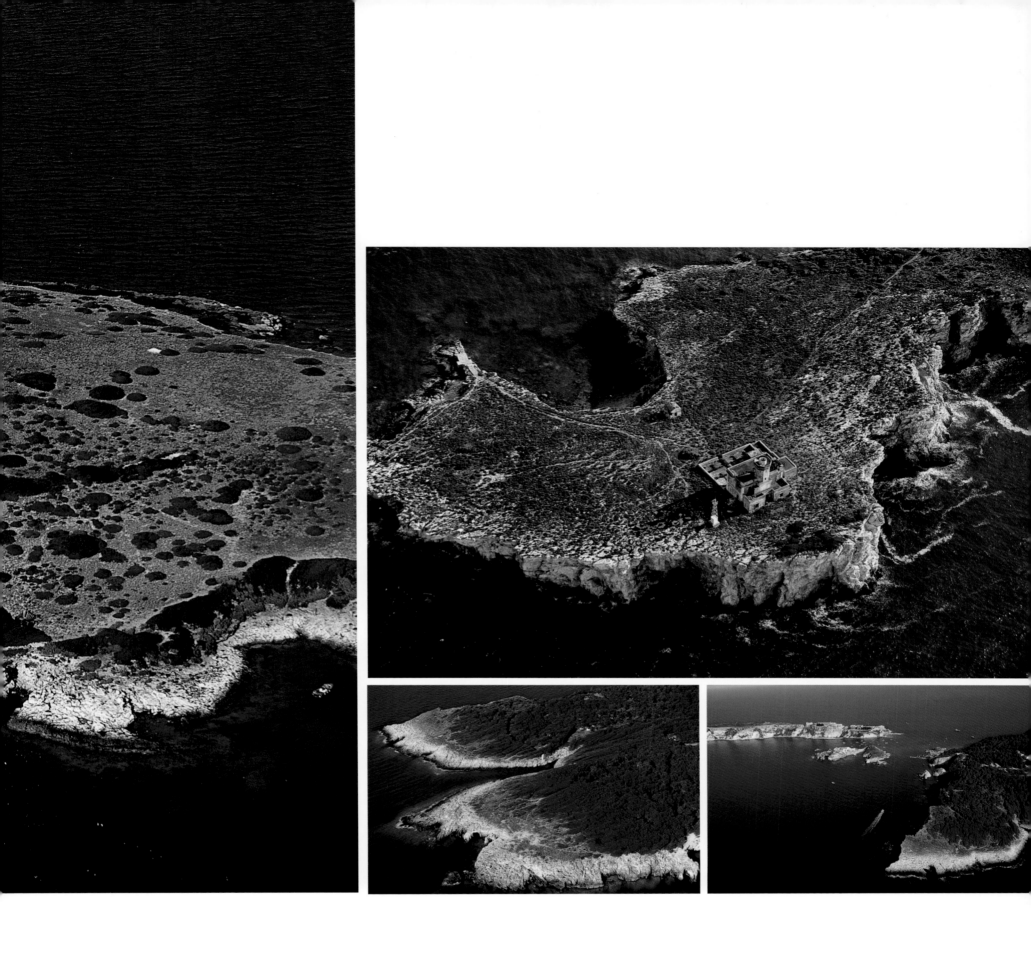

106 | Miramare Castle, with its elegant white silhouette, stands on a headland dominating the Gulf of Trieste.

Friuli Venezia Giulia – TRIESTE | The photograph shows a view of its great gardens that reach down to the seashore.

107 | A splendid path leads from Duino Castle, the elegant successor of the old fortified building

Friuli Venezia Giulia - ISTRIA | constructed in the 11th century, to Sistiana Bay, one of the pearls of Istria.

HIGH-ALTITUDE TREASURES

Italy's mountains are breathtaking granite monuments: peaks that rise above the clouds and volcanoes that resemble sleeping deities, but also serenely beautiful scenes – a frozen lake, a snow-covered forest, a green mountain pasture…

HIGH-ALTITUDE TREASURES

EUROPEAN PEAKS

109 | The Dent du Géant (left)
Valle d'Aosta – MONT BLANC MASSIF | is an imposing rocky spur
situated between the
Grandes Jorasses and
the Glacier du Géant that
towers over the snow-
capped ridge at its base.
The Grandes Jorasses
can be seen in the
background (right).

The dizziness of flight in some ways resembles the impression of bewilderment experienced when one is faced with the highest mountains. The air is rarified and the light clear, while the wind lashes the cockpit and shakes the fuselage, pushing the aircraft up and down and causing the pilot to brace himself at each rise and fall, before regaining control and checking the route. Flying over mountains seeking subjects to photograph requires not only nerves of steel, skill and a sense of awe, but also painstaking attention. The slightest mistake could be fatal, just as it could be to expert mountaineers. However, in return the mountain gods reward the daring with the wings and eyes of an eagle. The Alps offer thousands of pearls to photograph. They are a frontier and a limit of human existence, this may explain why the oldest barrier has never blocked anyone, but has always represented a place of exchange and life. The beauty of Europe's highest mountains has been handed down by reporters, oriental wise men and historians, while illustrators and landscape painters of the English-speaking world have vied with each other to depict the magnificence of the rock cathedrals. The Italian Alps are a maze of valleys and ridges, interrupted by striking scenery made up of waterfalls, lakes and snowy massifs that offer the aerial photographer the same evocative sensations that have fascinated generations of travelers over the centuries, as well as the sense of dizziness that only such images are able to generate. Our flight, following the same routes as the clouds that rush from west to east, offers extensive views that allow the extreme harmony of the Alpine system to be captured even if the diverse structural characteristics of the individual mountain chains correspond to different populations, cultures, regions and lifestyles.

Seen from above, the Valle d'Aosta resembles a great green riverbed, crammed with vegetation, with countless tributaries – the lateral valleys – constantly interrupting its course. The highest peaks of the continents stand guard at the end of the valleys. The Monte Rosa massif is a compendium of Alpine beauties: snowfields like seas, from which towers and pinnacles emerge; huge dark valleys that contrast with dazzling glaciers; granite peaks that rise above oceans of clouds, separating the world of the spirits from that of mortals. Our gaze runs along the Corno Nero, Castor and Pollux peaks, the glaciers and – lower down – the Gressoney, Ossola and Sesia valleys. The summit is crowned by a brown parallelepiped, a sort of arch of mankind, symbolizing the wish to dominate the peaks. This is Capanna Margherita, a magnificent work of engineering, anchored to slender Punta Gnifetti. The highest alpine refuge in Europe, at an altitude of 14,957 feet, is also a privileged observatory overlooking the surrounding forest of ice and granite.

A sunny day on the Matterhorn, the third-highest mountain of the Valle d'Aosta, on the Swiss border, is also a breathtaking spectacle: a blue sky shading into every possible tone of red at sunset provides the backdrop for the gigantic rocky pyramid, created especially to be flown over and around, following the trajectories traced by the eagles. From the air, the Matterhorn is a sheer stone blade without any terraces or steps, a monument to verticality, whose walls elude even the grip of snow and ice.

Then there's Mont Blanc: the noble, aristocratic Roof of Europe, which alternates wide flat spaces with dizzy peaks, between Italy and France – the Grand Plateau and the ridges of Mont Blanc du Tacul and Mont Maudit, the Brenva Spur and Glacier, the Grandes Jorasses and the Aiguilles that cut the clouds like razors grazing the blue sky. Finally, the most majestic, eastern face of Mont Blanc, simultaneously incredibly beautiful and repulsive: the Brenva face. It is a series of sharp rocky crests, sheer canyons and precarious hanging glaciers – tongues of ice that furrow the rock, falling straight from the peak and meeting in vast high-altitude amphitheaters or funnels, before breaking in imposing icefalls. An aerial tour of Mont Blanc also reveals the Grande Randonnée Trail: a magical Ariadne's thread, which unwinds between the Valle d'Aosta and Savoy, passing over tortuous glaciers, granite faces and pinnacles, lakes and waterfalls. However, it is also a journey into the deepest meaning of the mountains. The low-altitude world is distant and shadowed from these peaks, "genetically" removed from the bright light of the glaciers and the ethereal transparency of the air. Here the spirit flies free, reflecting itself in the greatness of the Earth's most impressive natural monuments. Mount Gran Paradiso, the dreamlike gentle mountain, with its verdant valleys and grassy uplands crossed by streams, can be seen from the massif, looking south beyond the Dora Baltea River, framed by imposing peaks. In the distance beyond, it is possible to make out the towering hieratic triangular peak of Mount Viso – the mother-mountain of the Po River Valley. Eastward, our flight is transformed into a fantastic voyage toward the striking Dolomite range. The gateway of the Eastern Alps is formed by the splendid Valtellina, flanked by the Bernina group and Mount Ortles, an immense massif covered with ice and snow and closed by the Stelvio, a magnificent high-altitude park inhabited by eagles and ibex. Trentino is heralded by the bare rock cathedrals of the Dolomites. The jagged peaks, blades, crests, pinnacles and breathtaking pink walls that tower over verdant meadows in summer and snowy white expanses in winter, have been defined as "stone gardens". Few mountains evoke the disturbing qualities of height and verticality as well as the Dolomites.

While the Alps gave birth to the Po River Valley and witnessed the history of the northern peoples, the Apennines have always formed the backbone of the peninsula. Although lower than the Alps, they are equally intricate and furrowed by valleys, offering untamed and surprising landscapes, as in the case of the Apuan Alps, which do not even reach 6,500 feet, but nonetheless boast high-altitude vistas, due to the marble quarries that whiten their slopes. The northern and central Apennines – sometimes wooded and sometimes bare and rocky – are sinuous in the section stretching from Liguria to Emilia and Tuscany, where their clay and sandstone origins are clearly apparent, while the Umbrian and Marchigian stretch emanates a sort of magical spirituality, which is summed up in the Gran Sasso, surrounded by the desert-like landscapes of Abruzzi. The southern mountains are rugged and at times spectral, with imposing limestone massifs or majestic volcanoes. The Calabrian chains and the Gennargentu in Sardinia offer the aerial photographer fairytale sights: the lakes iced-over following an unexpected winter frost, captured in La Sila massif; the wind that claws at the soft blanket of snow that whitens a forest on the Aspromonte massif; and the clouds that thin away around the peak of Mount Pollino, on the border with Basilicata. Gentle Vesuvius, which dominates the Naples plain, resembles a deity sleeping on its side; its history is inscribed in the Campi Flegrei (Phegraean Fields) and the folds of the land surrounding the crater, which reveal the ancient lava streams and explosions that claimed the lives of the inhabitants of Pompeii and Erculano. Etna, the ancient Sicilian giant, still displays continuous signs of activity and its red rivers are visible from the air, presenting as wounds on the volcano's flanks. The Montagnola, Monti Silvestri and huge skyward-gaping mouths of the three summit craters, are unforgettable highlights of a journey through the geological history of this part of Italy and, by extension, the entire Mediterranean.

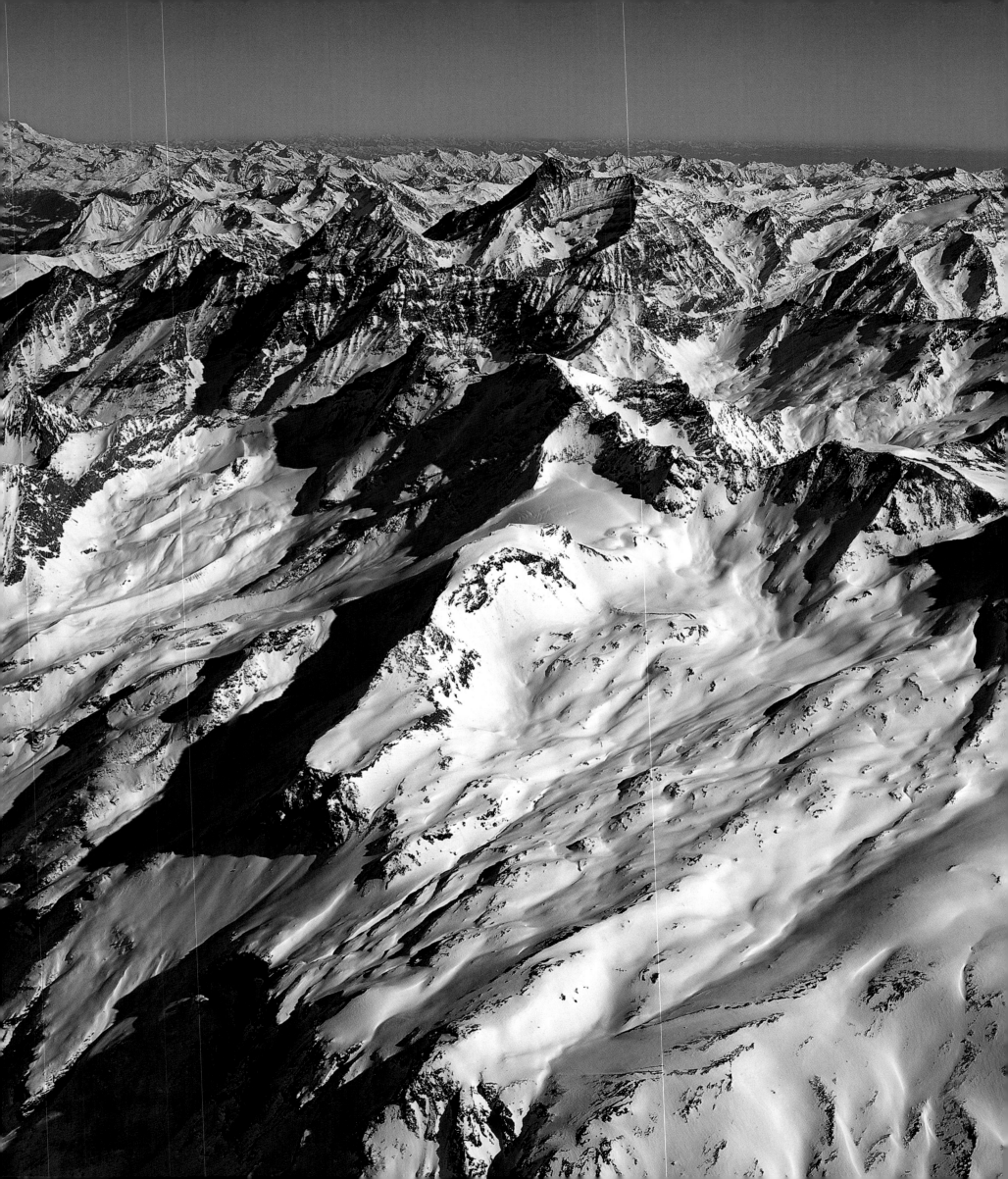

116-117 and 117 top
Valle d'Aosta – GRAIAN ALPS

This is the spectacle enjoyed by those flying over the Valle d'Aosta, from the regional capital towards the Mont Blanc massif: an unbroken chain of snowy peaks that constitute an authentic high-altitude paradise.

117 center and bottom
Piedmont/Valle d'Aosta – NORTHWESTERN ALPS

Piedmont and Valle d'Aosta are home to Europe's most majestic mountains. The impressive peaks include Mount Gran Paradiso (13,323 feet), situated between the two regions (center), and Mount Viso (12,602 feet), where the Po River rises from the eternal snows on the French border (bottom).

118 | Valle d'Aosta – MONT BLANC MASSIF | This breathtaking view of Europe's highest massif shows the Grandes Jorasses (left), the Dome de Rochefort and Mont Mallet (center and bottom) and the Aiguille de Rochefort (bottom left).

119 | Valle d'Aosta – MONT BLANC MASSIF | The Grandes Jorasses are among the most famous peaks of the massif and are situated on the border between Italy and France. These imposing stern granite summits are permanently covered with ice and snow. They reach a height of 13,806 feet and are considered a rock-climber's paradise.

120-121 | The Dent du Géant stands out against the blue sky of late winter. This impressive
Valle d'Aosta – MONT BLANC MASSIF | granite statue 13,166 feet high has been modeled by the wind and snow.

121 top | The Aiguille Noire de Peuterey rises above the clouds at an altitude of 12,379 feet close to the peak of Mont Blanc.
Valle d'Aosta – MONT BLANC MASSIF | The sheerness of its spurs and the constant risk of snowstorms have long made it a demanding training ground.

121 bottom | The peak of Mont Blanc (right) is characterized by a soft snowy cap, from which enormous permanent glaciers
Valle d'Aosta – MONT BLANC MASSIF | furrowed by seracs flow down the mountainside, like the Miage Glacier (left), entirely in Italian territory.

122-123
Piedmont – MOUNT CENIS

The sun and shadows play on the side of Mount Cenis, near Moncenisio Lake. Sand from the Sahara, transported by the wind on a meteorological whim, creates curious ocher-colored patterns on the frozen snow.

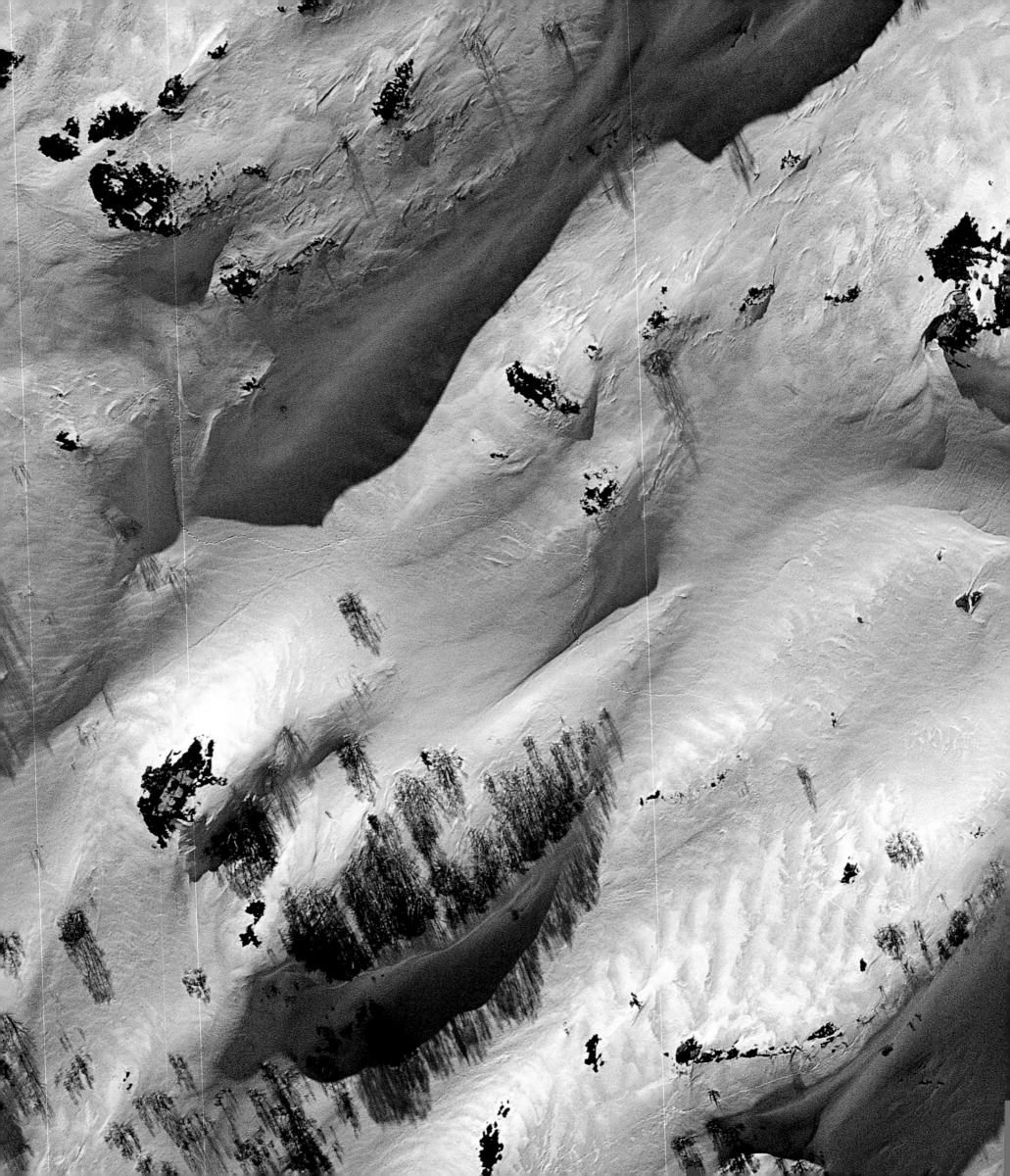

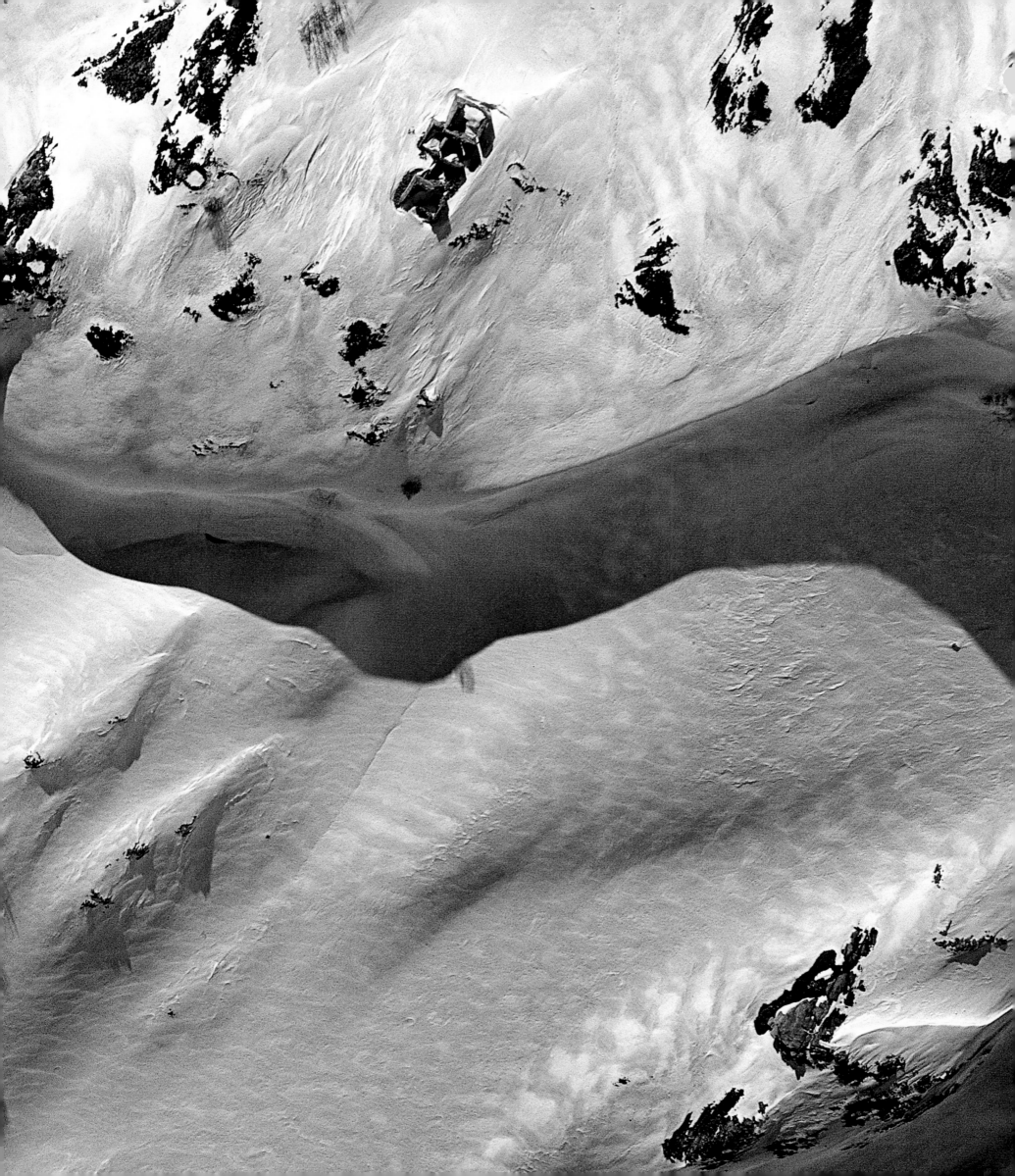

124-125 | Monte Rosa is the second most important massif in Europe in terms of size and the height of its
Piedmont – MONTE ROSA MASSIF | peaks, some of which are visible in this photograph: Signalkuppe, or Punta Gnifetti, (14,957 feet) with the
Capanna Margherita refuge (left), followed by Zumsteinspitze, Dufourspitze and Nordend.

125 | The warm light of dawn floods Signalkuppe (Punta Gnifetti) and the other Italian peaks of the Monte Rosa
Piedmont – MONTE ROSA MASSIF | group. The massif culminates in Dufourspitze (15,203 feet), the highest peak in Europe after Mont Blanc.

126-127
Piedmont – MONTE ROSA MASSIF

Seen from the high vantage point of Zumsteinspitze, the alpine refuge named after Queen Margherita appears an impossible work of man, balancing on the rocky ridge, overhanging a sea of ice. It was inaugurated in 1893, in honor of Queen Margherita of Savoy, and was completely rebuilt in 1980, using helicopters to transport the construction materials.

128-129
Piedmont – MONTE ROSA MASSIF

Capanna Margherita is the highest European mountain refuge and dominates the panorama of the Pennine Alps from a height of 14,957 feet. The landscape is thrilling and dizzying, made up of rock and ice, and dominated by the pyramidal form of the Matterhorn (center) and Mont Blanc (in the distance, left).

130-131
Valle d'Aosta – MATTERHORN | The Matterhorn (or Cervino, as it is known in Italy) projects its triangular shadow towards the horizon. It stands just over six miles from Monte Rosa, on the border with the Swiss canton of Valais. The jagged outline of the Dent Blanche stands out on the right of the picture.

131
Valle d'Aosta – MATTERHORN | The summit of the Matterhorn resembles the edge of a razorblade, making it difficult for snow to settle. At 14,692 feet high, it is the third-highest mountain in Europe. It was first conquered in 1865 by Edward Whymper, during a dramatic climb in which four of his team lost their lives.

132-133

Valle d'Aosta — MATTERHORN

The southern face of the Matterhorn is a dramatic and almost perpendicular tower, which rises above terrifying precipices. The pointed shape of the Swiss peak of Dent Blanche (14,295 feet) is visible on the left, still illuminated by the sun.

134 | The Catinaccio massif is an enormous buttress that effectively encapsulates the majesty and
Trentino Alto Adige – DOLOMITES | impressiveness of this range, despite the fact that it does not rise above 10,000 feet. The
Rosengartenspitze and, further right, the Vajolet Towers are clearly visible in the light of the setting sun.

135 | The Catinaccio, or Rosengarten ("Rose Garden"), group is located in the Siusi Alps, on the border
Trentino Alto Adige – DOLOMITES | between the Fassa and Gardena Valleys, between Moena and Ortisei. At sunset its rocks once again
become the "rose-covered" castle of the legendary King Laurin.

136-137 | Flying over the Catinaccio massif in winter, the huge expanse of snow that cloaks the peaks plays with the
Trentino Alto Adige – DOLOMITES | deep pink of the rocks at sunset. The distinctive semicircular silhouette of the Rosengartenspitze (9,780
feet) rises up in the distance, in the center of the photograph.

138-139 · Trentino Alto Adige – DOLOMITES | Seen from above, the Larsec Crags form a rocky cathedral, bristling with pinnacles. Cima Catinaccio and the northern Vajolet Towers can be seen in the distance, lit by the last rays of sun. One of the three Vajolet Towers - the Winkler - can be seen in the center, in the shadow.

139 · Trentino Alto Adige – DOLOMITES | The Vajolet Towers, in the center of the photograph, are vertical blocks of granite: the outermost spur, on the right, is named after Delago. The inner pinnacles appear united here, but are actually completely separate. The summits of the Catinaccio group stand all around, while the peak of the same name is visible behind the towers.

140-141
Trentino Alto Adige – DOLOMITES

The Sella massif is a huge, square, stratified mass characterized by wide terraces on which great snowfields form during the winter. It is situated at the meeting point of the Gardena, Fassa and Badia valleys and its summit stands at an altitude of 10,341 feet.

142-143
Trentino Alto Adige – DOLOMITES

The Pale di San Martino massif, whose highest peak - Cima Vezzana - reaches 10, 472 feet, rises above a sea of snow in the heart of the southern Dolomites, on the border between the provinces of Trento and Belluno, not far from the Marmolada. The photograph shows the great snowy plateau known as the Altopiano delle Pale, which covers an area of almost 20 square miles at an altitude of over 7,875 feet.

144 top
Veneto – DOLOMITES

Punta Rocca, one of the peaks of the Marmolada group is 10,856 feet high. It was first conquered by the English mountaineer John Ball around 1860. Alpine skiing enthusiasts can take advantage of a ski lift to Pian dei Fiacconi, where a spectacular snowy piste commences.

144 bottom and 145
Veneto – DOLOMITES

The Marmolada, on the border between Trentino and Veneto, between Agordino and the Fassa Valley, was the scene of fighting during the First World War. The dramatic peaks of the massif, dominated by Punta Penia (10,965 feet), are now a splendid setting for mountaineering enthusiasts.

146-147
Veneto – DOLOMITES

The photograph shows the almost vertical granite faces of Tofana di Rozes (10,581 feet), in the Ampezzo Dolomites, which make it a favorite destination for mountaineers wishing to tackle demanding Via Ferrata climbing.

148 top
Veneto – DOLOMITES | The spectacular Cristallo group, which rises in Cadore and dominates Cortina d'Ampezzo, is composed of the mountain of the same name (10,568 feet) and Piz Popena (10,341 feet), while a third subgroup is constituted by the Pomagagnon crest, divided from the main massif by the Padeon Valley.

148 bottom left and 149
Trentino Alto Adige –
DOLOMITES | The Sassolungo group, near Ortisei, reaches a height of 10,436 feet and belongs to the breathtakingly vertical Siusi Alps. Its gorges, faces and peaks offer incredibly beautiful views.

148 bottom center
Trentino Alto Adige – DOLOMITES | The peaks of the Pale di San Martino massif reach a height of 9,783 feet and form a lunar landscape of spires and pinnacles that soar into the sky of eastern Trentino.

148 bottom right
Trentino Alto Adige – DOLOMITES | The majestic Geisler/Odle group in the Funes Valley, set in a great natural park, raises its rocky pinnacles to heights of up to 8,202 feet.

150 | The Brenta group is commonly subdivided into three sectors, which are arranged along a north-south axis for
Trentino Alto Adige – DOLOMITES | approximately 26 miles, covering an area of around 155 square miles. It alternates gentle landscapes with dizzy
views. A single system of connecting Via Ferrata routes enables mountaineers to cross the entire group.

150-151 | The Brenta Dolomites are world-famous for their spectacular vertical rock faces and enormous peaks
Trentino Alto Adige – DOLOMITES | that rise from a sea of permanent ice. The highest summits exceed 10,000 feet, reaching 10,410 feet at
the Cima Tosa (center), which separates the Sole and Non valleys.

152-153
Trentino Alto Adige – DOLOMITES Illuminated by the golden rays of the setting sun, the granite peaks of the Sfulmini chain in the Brenta group recall a majestic Gothic cathedral, soaring skyward.

152
Trentino Alto Adige – DOLOMITES One of the most prestigious mountains to scale in the Dolomites is Crozzon di Brenta (10,285 feet), a stately peak belonging to the southern sector of the group.

154-155
Tuscany – APUAN ALPS | The mountains around the marble "capitals" of Massa and Carrara are the source of the famous white stone. The so-called "Marble Trails", used by the quarriers since ancient times, cross this part of the Apennines winding from Mount Altissimo towards Carrara and Versilia. These quarries were the source of the precious stone that constituted the raw material for Michelangelo's most famous sculptures.

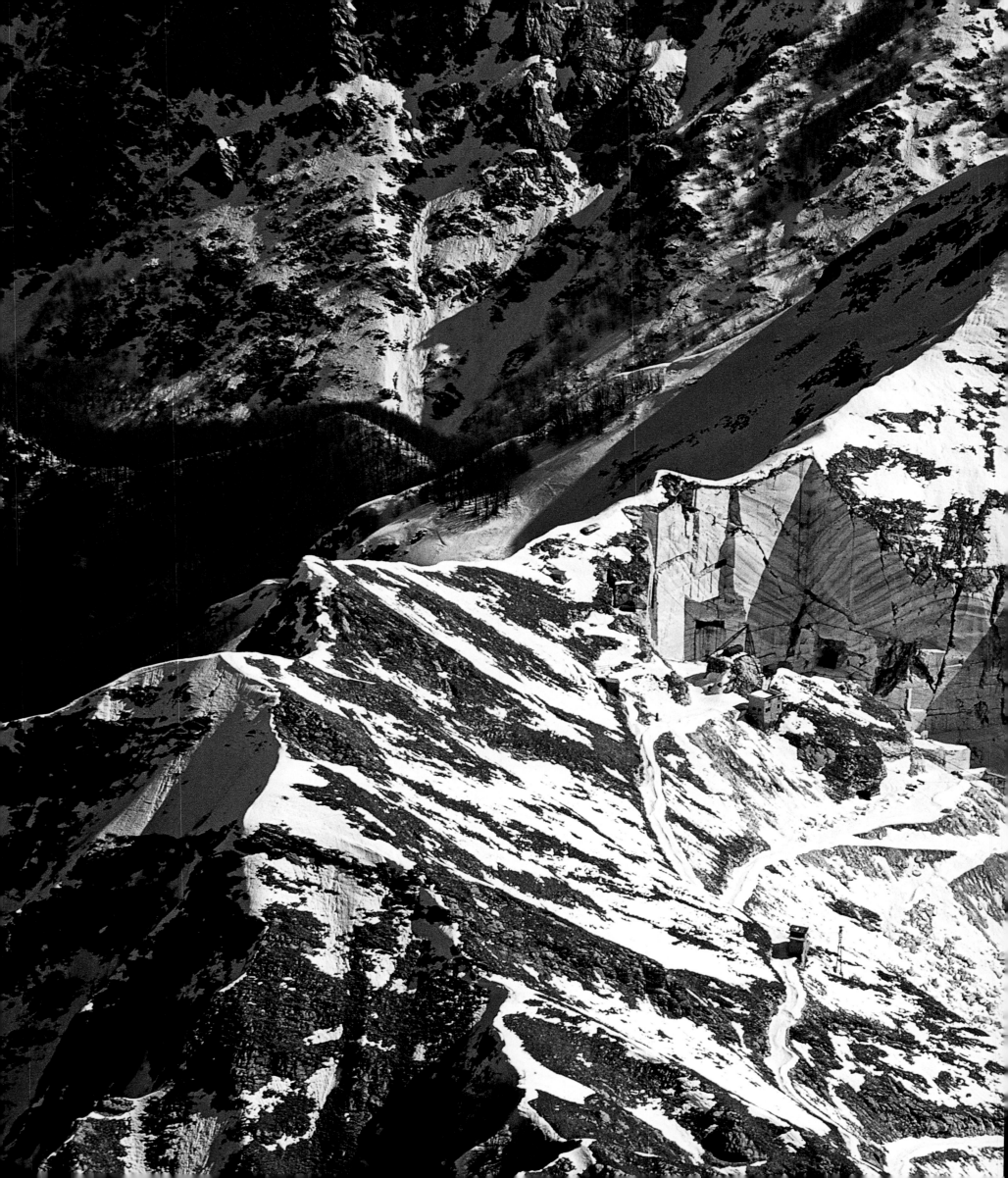

156-157
Tuscany – **TUSCAN-EMILIAN APENNINES**

This winter view of the slopes of Mount Abetone, shows the Tuscan-Emilian Apennines covered with the first, light blanket of snow. This side of the Apennines is overlooked by the highest peak – Mount Cimone (7,103 feet), which slopes down towards the Emilian plain.

157
Abruzzo – MAJELLA MASSIF | The peaks of the Majella massif can be glimpsed between the fluffy clouds. This mountain system, dominated by Monte Amaro (9,760 feet), is an arm of the Abruzzo Apennines that slopes down towards the sea.

158-159
Tuscany - APUAN ALPS | The trees of this forest and the shadows cast by the grazing light create a closely-woven pattern on the fresh snow. The Apuan Alps run parallel to the Tuscan-Emilian Apennines, reaching an altitude of over 6,500 feet.

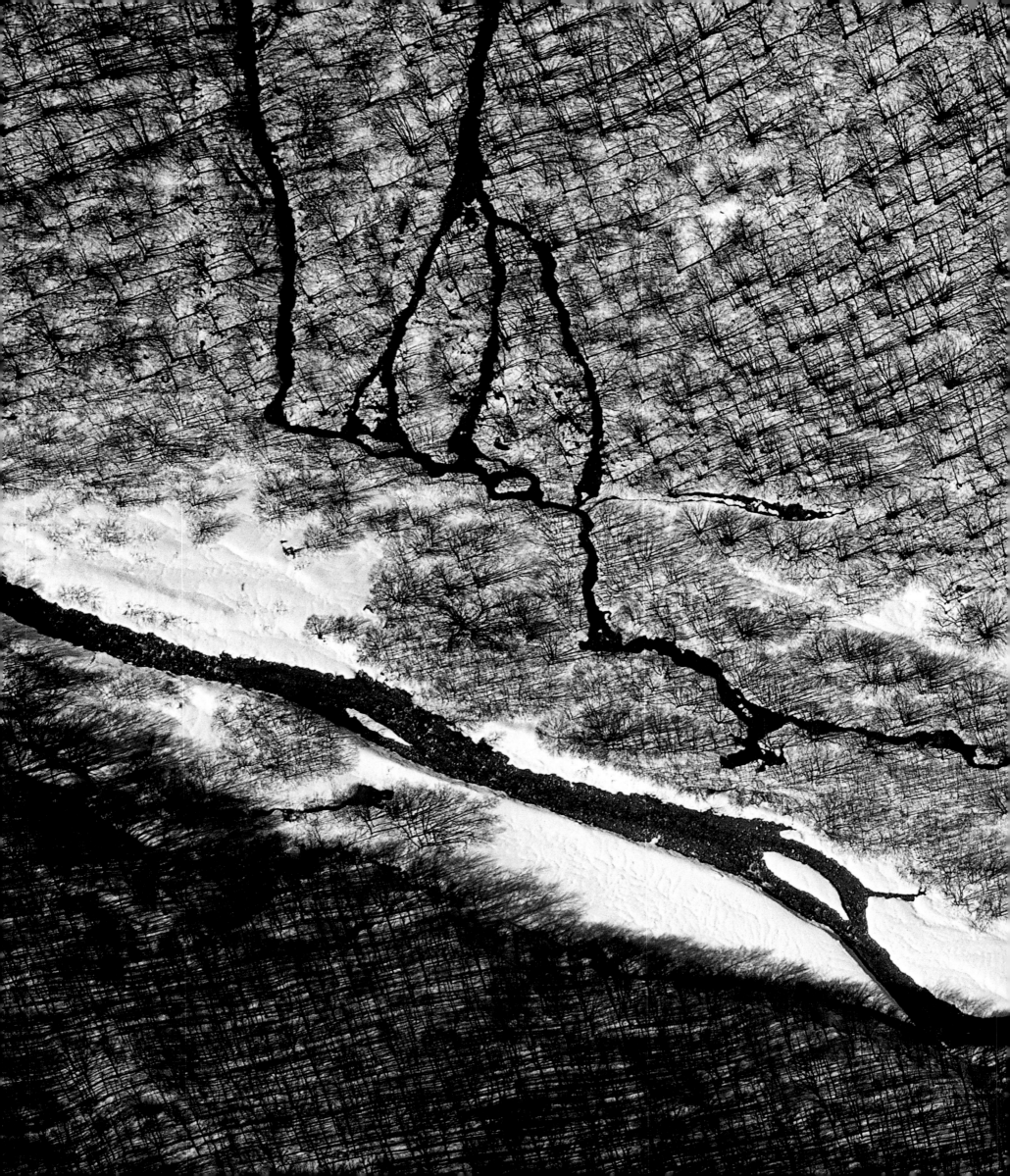

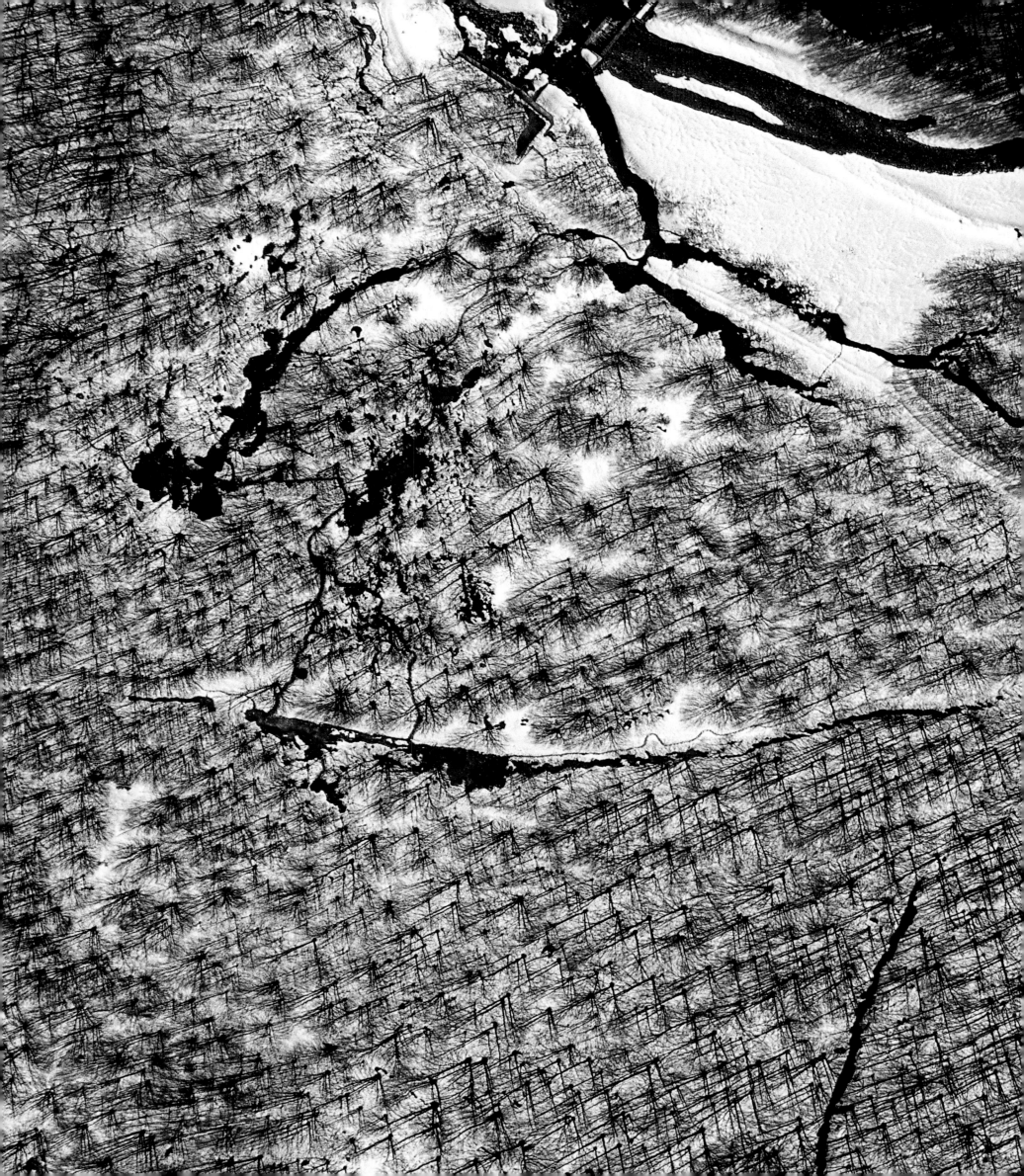

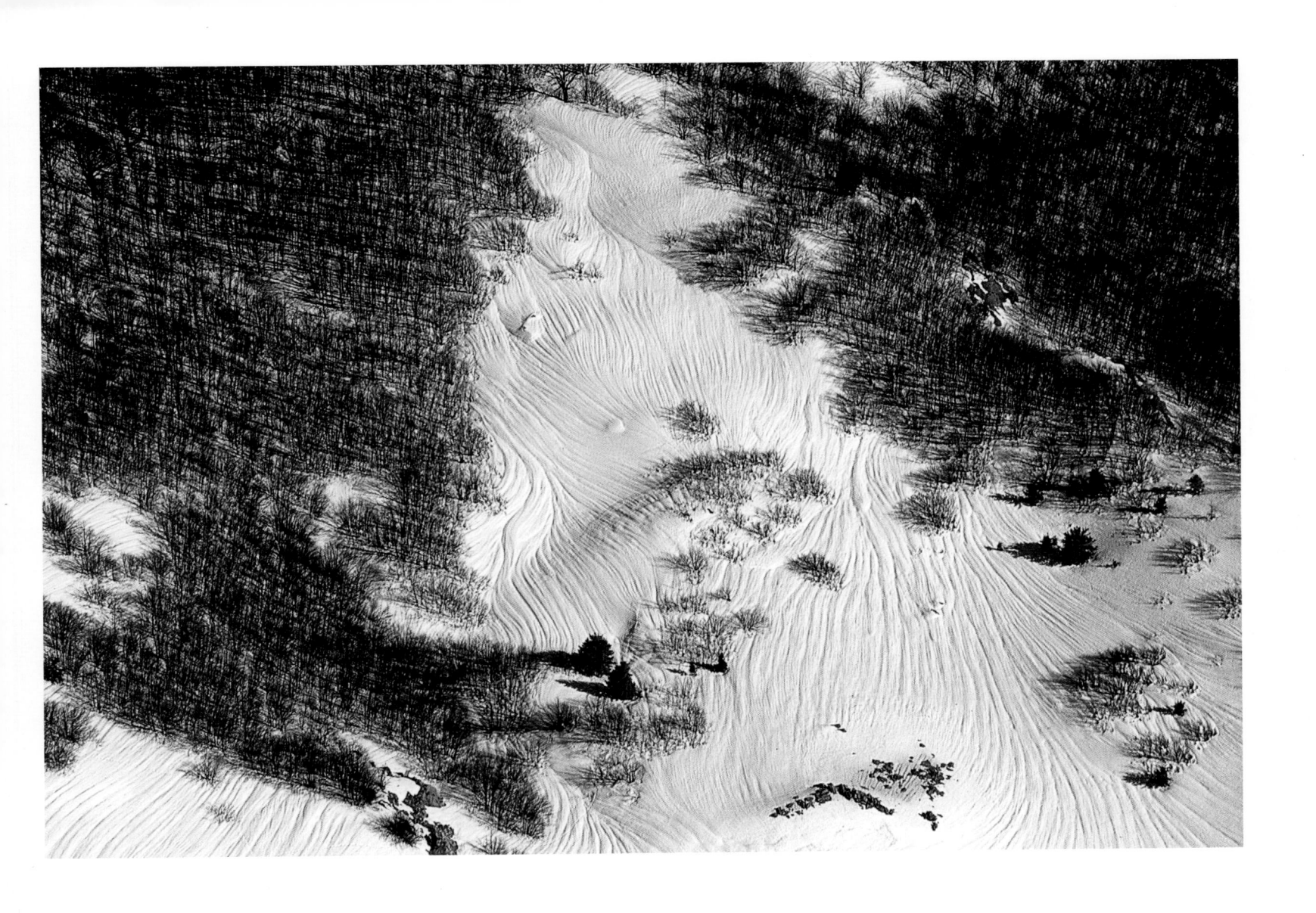

160 and 161
Emilia-Romagna – TUSCAN-EMILIAN APENNINES

An immaculate white sea of foam appears to descend from this larch wood towards the valley. The snow on this side of the Apennines has been modeled like a thick ivory mane. The magical effect has been created by the fierce winds that blow at these altitudes. The Tuscan-Emilian stretch is the longest of the various sections into which the Apennines are conventionally divided. This rocky backbone extends over 800 miles along the entire peninsula, from Liguria to Calabria.

162 top and bottom

CENTRAL – Abruzzo/Lazio
APENNINES

The mountains of central Italy offer surprising landscapes: from the bare, weathered rock of the Abruzzo Mountains (above) to the gentle snowy peaks of the Reatini range, which includes Mount Terminillo (below) that rises to a height of 7,260 feet.

162 center and 162-163

Abruzzo – GRAN SASSO

The Gran Sasso National Park is home to chamois, roe deer, wolves, wildcats, stone martens and weasels and acts as a hinge territory between the northern and Mediterranean regions. The only glacier in southern Europe is situated amid the stately peaks of the massif, which reach heights of over 9,500 feet.

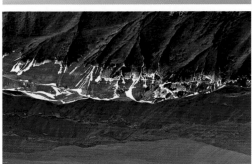

164-165
Campania – VESUVIUS
Vesuvius is an active, although not extinct, volcano. It has a history of spectacular eruptions, as testified by its enormous summit crater. The edge of the crater is home to several observatories that monitor the volcano and attempt to predict when it will next erupt.

164
Campania – VESUVIUS
Vesuvius stands between the Tyrrhenian Sea and the Irpinia Mountains. Its spectacular position can be seen in this photograph, showing the Bay of Naples and Castellamare di Stabia (left), with the Sorrento Peninsula in the background.

167 | On the border between Calabria
Calabria – POLLINO | and Basilicata, the Pollino
National Park, with the Pollino
and Orsomarso massifs, offers
visitors memorable views and an
extremely varied flora and fauna.

166-167 | This statue of Christ the Redeemer, surrounded by snow, was erected 6,417 feet above sea level, on the summit of Montalto, also known as
Calabria – ASPROMONTE | Mount Cocuzza, the highest peak of the Aspromonte massif. Aspromonte forms the southernmost tip of the Apennines and radiates down
towards the sea in an intricate system of peaks and untamed valleys, which are home to wolves, wild boar and eagles.

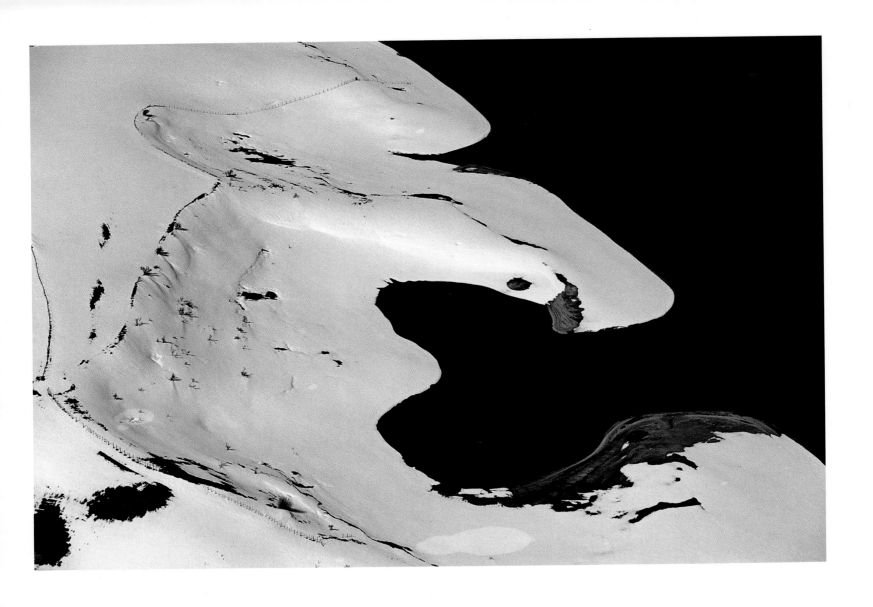

168, 169 and 170-171 | La Sila massif, a crystalline granite plateau in northern Calabria with altitudes ranging between 3,600
Calabria – LA SILA | and 5,500 feet is scattered with artificial lakes, created during the 1920s, which are practically
inaccessible in winter, and thus all the more evocative. The photograph on the right shows a boat
abandoned on the edge of Lake Ampollino after its waters have retreated and frozen.

172-173 | Etna is the highest and most important volcano in the Mediterranean region. Its summit craters are situated at an
Sicily – ETNA | altitude of 10,902 feet and are often covered with snow. The outskirts of Catania, clinging to the slopes of the volcano,
can be glimpsed on the far left, while the Erei Mountains are visible on the right.

THEATERS OF ART AND HISTORY

The throbbing hearts of ancient Italy are now the nerve and communication centers of a country that lives for the future, without forgetting the past. Its cities have thus retained the elegance, monuments and sometimes also the compact beauty of former days.

THEATERS OF ART AND HISTORY

ANCIENT COMMUNES

Piazza del Comune is the artistic and historic center of Cremona. It is overlooked by open galleries and precious monuments, including the 13th-century Baptistery, with its typical octagonal plan.

Modern-day Italy is the direct heir of the Italy of the Communes. In no other place in the world has history created so many independent cultural entities, breaking down and dividing up the territory into numerous small segments, which have devised original and varied urban, artistic and architectural solutions. The smaller cities, in both northern and central Italy, have often preserved their Roman plan, which was fortified and altered during the Middle Ages and embellished – when conditions permitted – during the Renaissance. A good example is Aosta, which the Romans called Augusta Praetoria: the square plan of the old *castrum*, city walls, Arch of Augustus, Roman theater, amphitheater and Church of Sant'Orso can all be clearly seen from the air. Turin, the aristocratic capital of the Kingdom of Savoy, whose heritage is similar to that of Aosta. It resembles an old, but still attractive lady, who is happy to pose with the family jewels. Seen from the air, ancient Augusta Taurinorum is a crossroads of elegant palaces, long, straight tree-lined avenues, extensive parks modeled on their French counterparts, two intersecting rivers and a hill that attenuates the impact of the city. However, Turin is also factories, integrated in the urban fabric or surrounded by the harmonious development of the metropolis, and sumptuous suburbs, dotted with splendid aristocratic residences. Examples are the Venaria Reale and Stupinigi palaces, set in splendid grounds, whose large and well-manicured lawns ringed by woods the size of villages appear from above as orderly green patches. Beyond the barrier of the Maritime Alps is Genoa – another noble city currently enjoying a revival, which snakes its way along the narrow strip of land suitable for building between the fortified high ground and the wide gulf. Its skeleton is constituted by the narrow streets of the historic district and the maze of alleys, while its backbone is formed by the overpass that cuts through the heart of the city, running parallel to the coast. An aerial review clearly conveys the dual personality of the port for the Genoese, a source of wealth, yet also a physical and mental barrier between the city and the sea. Moving away from the Mediterranean toward the Alps and flying back over the Apennines, a practically uninterrupted sequence of towns heralds the gray urban sprawl of Italy's modern business capital. Milan is a reticular expanse of streets and houses, which thicken around its individual municipalities, before thinning into unexpected areas of farmland, a remnant of the 19th-century city, until reaching the innermost rings of the city, where the green parks and avenues are overwhelmed by the gray stone and concrete. Old and new masterpieces of architecture emerge from the sea of houses of this art city: the spires of the Duomo, the Pirelli Tower, the Castello Sforzesco and the Basilica of Sant'Ambrogio. The crawling traffic makes the city resemble a living organism, breathing rapidly and ceaselessly. The main streets that start in the center of Milan stretch outward, toward the suburbs and beyond, to the wealthy and chaotic provinces of Lombardy: Pavia, with its incomparable Certosa (Carthusian Monastery), Brescia, Bergamo, Mantua, Cremona. A network of roads penetrates the valleys, toward Sondrio, Lake Maggiore and Lake Como, as well as Veneto and Emilia. Gray routes flank the blue ones of canals and rivers, branching into ever-smaller lines, until reaching Venice, with its magical houses built on piles. A dreamlike network of *calli*, little piazzas, canals and bridges stretches over the water from Ca' Pesaro to Rialto Bridge and from Palazzo Grassi to St. Mark's square. Venice from the air appears as a closely-knit web of old streets mixed with green canals. South of Venice, the cities are marked by red roofs and unexpected monumental squares, immersed in the greenery of the seemingly endless countryside. Bologna, the rich capital of Emilia, is a synthesis of the harmony and vitality displayed by the Italian regions as we move toward the center of the peninsula, with its geometric arcades, of marble and sandstone that contrast with its medieval towers. On the other side of the Apennines, Florence is the epitome of beauty and elegance. Its gentle hills converge in the purest jewels of art: from the Uffizi and Palazzo Vecchio to the Church of Santa Maria Novella and the Ponte Vecchio, in a sea of red roofs, dominated by Giotto's Campanile and Brunelleschi's dome. The Arno winds its way between elegant gardens and avenues lined with pine, plane and cypress tress, spanned by a succession of monumental bridges. Florence, more than Bologna, is the gateway to central Italy in which the beauties of art and nature seem to permeate each other. The quintessential natural spirituality that inspired great works of engineering can be found in green Umbria with its rugged hills and austere medieval cities: Gubbio, Perugia, Orvieto, Todi and Assisi are pure magic and enchantment. The cities of the Lazio coast live in the shadow of the great capital, but from the air appear as little gems, whose harmony is hardly touched by the turbulent development of their chaotic suburbs. Not even the great eye of aerial photography can manage to encompass Rome – the city of the seven hills, the Roman forums and the popes. The city has many faces: the archaeological sites, the Vatican City, the lower-class 15th-century districts, the great cathedrals and small churches, the flower-covered terraces amid the low roofs, the green avenues that accompany the Tiber on its slow course between the artistic and historic monuments, the new city of Fascist imperialism, and the immense metropolis of the suburbs that run along the ancient imperial roads. This cultural dimension resulting from centuries of splendor is practically impossible to capture from the sky. We will thus content ourselves with admiring the marvelous fresco of this colossal capital immersed in greenery, where marble, squares and monuments happily coexist. Our southward flight passes over the fascinating Bay of Naples, whose waters lap one of Europe's most mysterious and intricate cities. Its alleys, palaces, villas and illegal housing reach as far as the slopes of Vesuvius. Naples has been the scene of many plays and each of their actors has played a role in history. This explains the apparent contradictoriness of the city plan, which creates a sense of dizziness in the visitor when seen from above – from the Maschio Angioino to Capodimonte, passing through the lively lower-class district of the old city. The same impression is experienced by the photographer looking down on Bari. Although now a modern city, its historical district is made up of such closely-packed, branching streets as to resemble a labyrinth with no way out. All the cities of southern Italy bear the signs of the events of thousands of years. The main Sardinian cities, from Nuoro to Cagliari, have an old nucleus squeezed between the sea, hills and inland lagoons, while the ancient Greek origins of the Calabrian and Sicilian cities are still clearly visible and form the basis for the complex layers of history and architecture left by the Normans, Arabs and Bourbons. The magnificence of Palermo's aristocratic past is summed up in its great cathedral and charming botanical gardens, which embellish what has become a metropolis, comprised of old working-class districts and sprawling new residential areas. Catania's rapid growth seems to be fueled by the volcanic energy of Etna, as it greedily consumes the free space between the deep blue sea and the scorched countryside populated by prickly pears.

180
Lombardy — MILAN
The Castello Sforzesco, a fortified palace that is now home to museums and cultural institutes, is one of Milan's most evocative monuments. The Renaissance castle is actually a collection of varied styles, each of which is the legacy of a different period.

181
Lombardy — MILAN
The majestic soaring Arco della Pace is one of Milan's greatest 19th-century monuments. It was erected by order of Napoleon, who desired a memorial that would celebrate his triumphs. However, construction proceeded slowly and the arch was not completed until 1838.

182-183
Lombardy — MILAN
Along with the Basilica of Sant'Ambrogio, the cathedral is undoubtedly Milan's most important religious monument. It was commenced by Gian Galeazzo Visconti in the 14th century, but several of its distinctive features – such as the façade and main spire – were not defined until the 18th and 19th centuries.

184-185
Lombardy — MILAN
This photograph clearly shows the cross-shaped plan of the Galleria Vittorio Emanuele, inaugurated in 1867 and completed in 1878. Its center is topped by a glass dome supported by an iron frame, inspired by similar structures built in Paris and London.

186-187
Lombardy – MILAN | Milan's Stazione Centrale is one of the largest railway stations in Europe. It was officially inaugurated in 1931 to replace the old 19th-century Stazione Centrale. Its 650-foot wide monumental façade overlooks Piazza Duca d'Aosta.

187 | Porta Orientale, subsequently
Lombardy – MILAN | renamed Porta Venezia, stands
on the spot in which the city
once opened onto the Brianza
countryside. Today the frenzied
urban growth of the metropolis
has left it practically in the city
center, at the meeting point of
important streets.

188-189 | Founded by Saint Ambrose in 379 AD, the
Lombardy – MILAN | basilica that bears his name has retained
part of its original austere appearance,
although its current form is heavily influenced
by extensive work that was carried out
during the 12th and, in particular, 19th
centuries.

190 | The Gran Madre di Dio Church was inspired by the Pantheon in Rome and was built in the 1830s near the
Piedmont – TURIN | bank of the Po to celebrate the return of Vittorio Emanuele I following the Congress of Vienna. A legend
claims that Holy Grail is housed in the crypt of the building.

191 | The great dome of the Mole Antonelliana is the symbol of Turin. It was built between 1863 and 1889 by the architect Alessandro
Piedmont – TURIN | Antonelli and was originally intended to be a synagogue. Almost 550 feet tall, it is now home to the National Museum of Cinema.

192 | Palazzo Madama was built in the heart of the city during the 17th century. Despite its Baroque façade
Piedmont – TURIN | and monumental staircase, designed by Filippo Juvarra, its layout is very similar to a medieval castle.

193 | The statue of the Standard Bearer of the Sardinian Army, presented to Turin by the city of Milan in 1857, stands in the
Piedmont – TURIN | center of Piazza Castello. It is one of the many signs of the city's past as the Savoy capital.

194-195 | Piazza Castello was planned in the 16th century and is the very heart of Turin. Palazzo Madama (right) and the Royal
Piedmont – TURIN | Palace with the Cathedral (top left) are visible in the photograph. The Prefecture, Royal Armory and Teatro Regio
opera house also overlook the square, which is lined with arcades housing stores and the city's historic cafés.

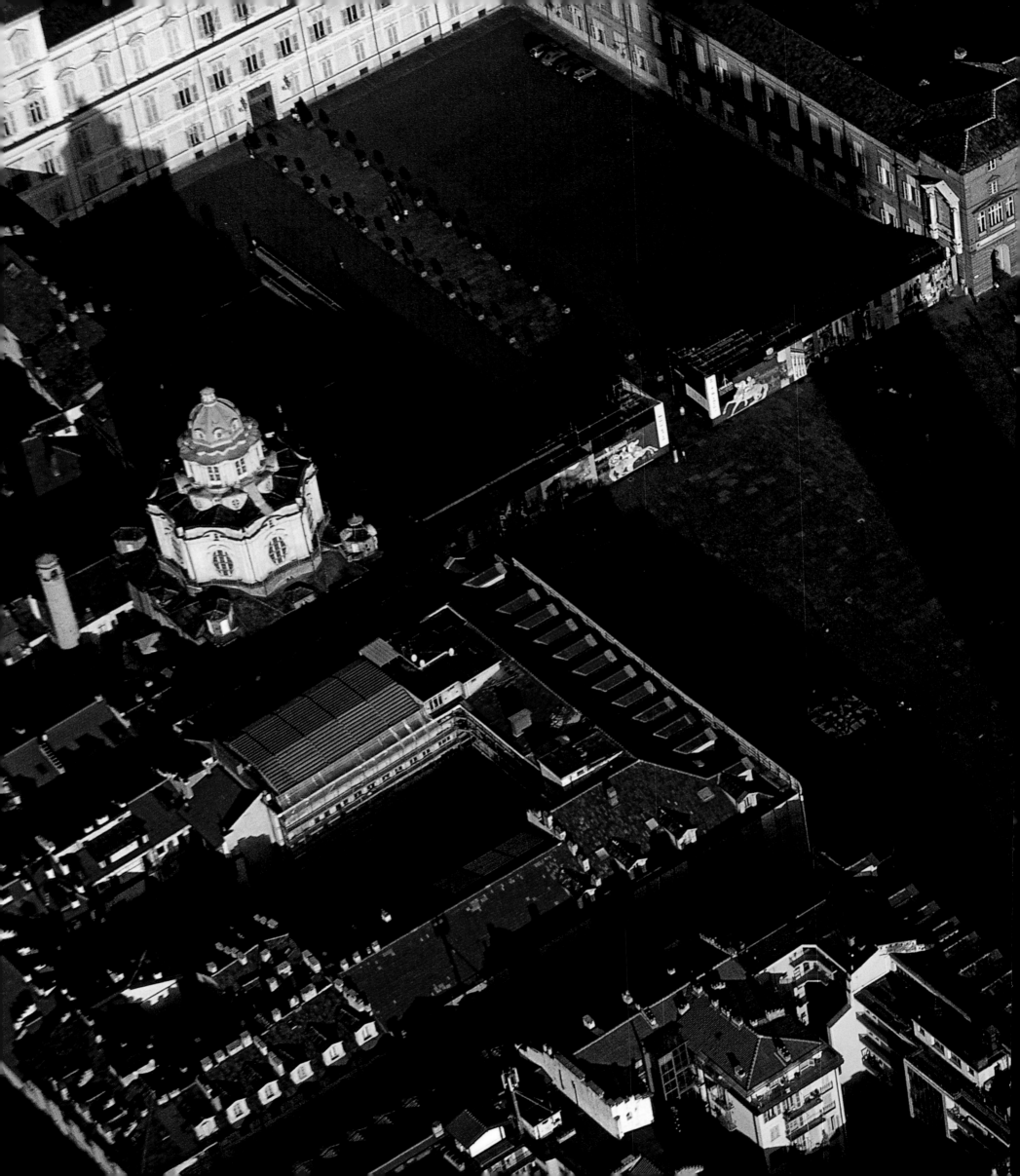

196 | The Royal Hunting Lodge at Stupinigi is one of Juvarra's masterpieces. It was built just a few miles
Piedmont – TURIN | from the center of Turin, to which it is connected by an evocative avenue, and is now home to the
Museum of Art and Furniture.

197 | The Basilica of Superga, like many of Turin's monuments, was designed by the great architect Juvarra. This Baroque masterpiece was
Piedmont – TURIN | long the burial place of the Savoy family, and its 245-foot dome dominates the hill of the same name on the western outskirts of Turin.

198-199
Liguria – GENOA | Palazzo San Giorgio was built in 1260 by Brother Oliviero, by order of Simon Boccanegra, the Capitano del Popolo. The palace served as the city hall until 1262. According to legend, Marco Polo dictated his *Travels* to Rustichello da Pisa in the building's dungeons.

199

Liguria – GENOA

Past and present mingle and overlap in Genoa. The historic Piazza della Vittoria, with the Arco dei Caduti war memorial (top), and the suburb of Boccadasse (bottom) contrast with new attractions, such as the port (center). Futuristic buildings and radical renovations made during the 1990s have transformed the port into a state-of-the-art trade fair area.

The layout and most illustrious monuments of the ancient and powerful diocese of Vercelli reveal important traces of the city's noble past. This panoramic view shows the 16th-century cathedral (left) and, above all, the Basilica of Sant'Andrea (bottom), a splendid example of the 13th-century Romanesque-Gothic style.

Piazza Ducale (top), the center of Vigevano, has Renaissance origins. It was built in 1494 by Lodovico il Moro as a monumental entrance to the castle (right), the summer residence of the Sforza court, and was purportedly designed by Leonardo da Vinci.

202
Lombardy – BRESCIA, MANTUA AND PAVIA

The three cities of the Po River Valley are home to old universities and are important cultural centers studded with precious architectural gems: the 15th-century Loggia and piazza of the same name in Brescia (top); the Castello di San Giorgio in Mantua (center); the cathedral in Pavia (bottom).

203
Lombardy – COMO

The enchanting city of Como, set on the shores of the lake of the same name, has an important medieval historic district, a magnificent cathedral (center) and elegant private villas lining the waterside.

204-205
Lombardy – PAVIA

The Certosa of Pavia is a Renaissance masterpiece that was commenced in 1396 (but not finished until 1473) by Gian Galeazzo Visconti as a family mausoleum.

Piazza Matteotti, in the center of Udine, boasts a handsome fountain and Renaissance buildings. The former marketplace vies with Piazza Libertà as the "emblem" of the Friuli city.

207 bottom | Piazza dell'Unità d'Italia reflects the glorious past of Trieste. It was formerly known as Piazza Grande but was
Friuli Venezia Giulia – TRIESTE | renamed Piazza dell'Unità d'Italia in 1918. Today it is a rendezvous point for the lively local scene.

206 center and 206-207 | Piazza delle Erbe, built on the ancient site of the Roman forum (small photograph), and the Arena, an amphitheater
Veneto – VERONA | capable of holding 25,000 spectators that dates back to the 1st century AD (right in the large photograph), are the twin
focuses of life in Verona, the splendid city on the banks of the Adige, famous for the romantic story of Romeo and Juliet.

208 | The Basilica of Santa Giustina is Padua's largest church and is distinguished by its campanile, eight
Veneto – PADUA | domes and unfinished façade. It was destroyed by an earthquake during the 12th century and was
subsequently remodeled several times before assuming its current colossal form in the 16th century.

209 | The Basilica of Sant'Antonio is Padua's most important religious center and attracts pilgrims from all over Italy. Its simple
Veneto – PADUA | Lombard Romanesque brick façade is dominated by eight gray Byzantine-style domes.

Venice is a feast for the eyes, with a wealth of surprising views: distinctive tapering gondolas, ideal for plying the city's narrow canals (top), calli, canals, bridges, small squares (like Piazza San Giacomo, bottom) and aristocratic palaces (such as the Ca' d'Oro, center).

210-211

Veneto – VENICE

Seen from the air, Venice is an elegant and never chaotic mass of old houses, magically held together by the city's eternal charm. This panorama shows the splendid palaces that line the Grand Canal and St. Mark's Square (top), which stands opposite the island of San Giorgio.

212-213

Veneto – VENICE

The enchanting city of Venice, already a settlement of extraordinary pile-dwellings in the 5th century, sits on the lagoon in a dreamy maze of streets and canals. It is divided into two by the Grand Canal, with the districts of Cannaregio, San Marco and Castello to the north (on the left of the photograph) and those of Santa Croce, San Polo and Dorsoduro to the south (right). In the distance it is possible to discern the islands of Giudecca (top right), San Giorgio (top center) and the Lido (top, almost on the edge of the photograph).

214 | St. Mark's Basilica, built in the 11th century, is Venice's most important religious center. The building shows
Veneto – VENICE | clear Byzantine influences, which are evident in its profusion of decorative elements and its Greek cross
plan, emphasized by five domes – one at the crossing of the arms and four at the ends. For many
centuries the basilica was the chapel of the Doges and the scene of their presentation to the people.

215 | The marble piazza of St. Mark's Square is one of the world's most famous urban spaces and lies between St. Mark's
Veneto – VENICE | Basilica, the Doges' Palace, the Campanile, Jacopo Sansovino's Libreria Vecchia, the Procuratie Vecchie and Nuove, the
Correr Museum and the Clock Tower. It branches out into the "Piazzetta" known as "il Broglio" at the meeting point of
monumental Venice and the lagoon.

216-217 | St. Mark's Square is dominated by the 325-foot Campanile that dates back to the 10th century and is bound on the east
Veneto – VENICE | by St. Mark's Basilica and the Doges' Palace (center of photograph). This palace is the symbol of Venetian glory and
former residence of the Doges. It was built in the 12th century and modified during later periods. Today it is a graceful
porticoed building, clad with pink and white marble, which is connected to the old prisons by the famous Bridge of Sighs.

218 | Veneto – VENICE | The Church of Santa Maria della Salute, at the entrance to the Grand Canal from the lagoon, dates back to the 17th century and forms a marble white patch in the midst of Venice's red roofs. Towards the lagoon beyond is the point formed by the Dogana da Mar.

219 | Veneto – VENICE | The Church of Santa Maria della Salute was built in the 17th century as a votive offering in memory of the terrible 1630 plague epidemic that swept Europe and decimated the city. The Baroque-style building has an unmistakable octagonal plan.

220
Veneto – VENICE

The Grand Canal crosses the entire city like a majestic and monumental "water highway". The most famous of the bridges that span its length is undoubtedly the Rialto, situated in the heart of the city's old commercial district. It connects the district of San Marco with that of San Polo and opens onto the vegetable market (Erberia) and fish market (Pescheria), which are still picturesque and lively spots today.

221
Veneto – VENICE

Rialto Bridge is one of Venice's most famous monuments and was built between 1588 and 1592 by Antonio da Ponte. Its "humpback" design allowed an armed galley to pass beneath it. It has always been crossed by a street lined with shops.

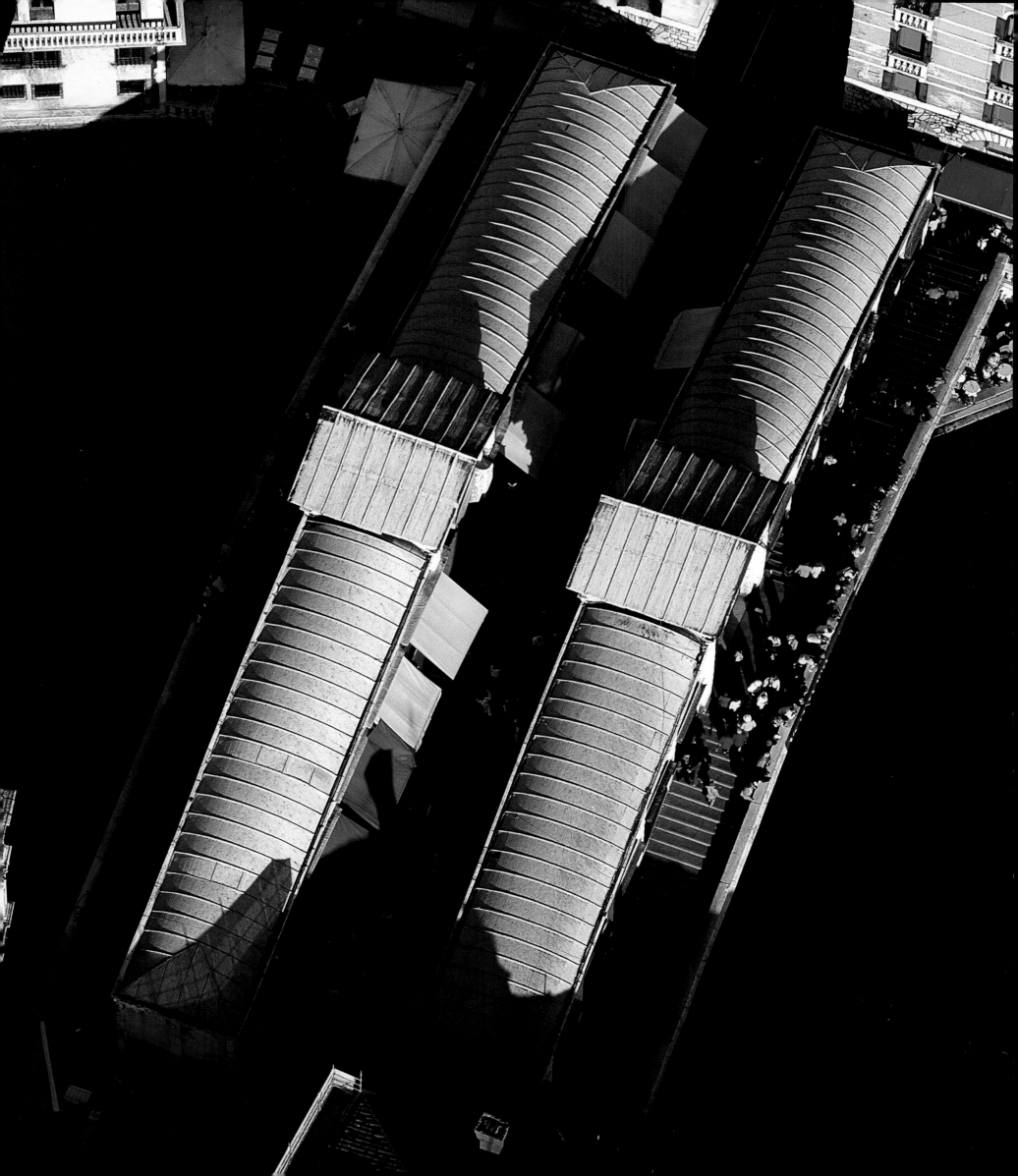

222 top
Emilia Romagna - FERRARA

Ferrara is dotted with the traces of its former Este rulers. The city's refined elegance is clearly visible in its principal monuments: the Cathedral, Palazzo Schifanoia, Palazzo dei Diamanti and the Castle. Even the plan, with its broad streets and elegant gardens, contributes to heightening the charm of this great Renaissance city.

222 center, bottom and 222-223
Emilia Romagna - RAVENNA

Ravenna, considered the Byzantium of the West, is an ancient imperial city that is home to the majestic testimonials of early Christian art. The Church of Sant'Apollinare in Classe (opposite, center) is a magnificent example of religious architecture. It was consecrated in 549 AD and its interior embellished with precious mosaics during the 6th and 7th centuries. A cylindrical campanile was added in the 11th century. The Church of San Vitale (large photograph), completed in 547, shares the main characteristics of Sant'Apollinaire: a bare brick exterior and dazzlingly sumptuous interior. However, Ravenna is also a rich and lively city, with squares where people gather (opposite, bottom, Piazza del Popolo) reflecting its high quality of life.

224-225
Emilia Romagna – PARMA | Parma is a handsome city with a modern pace and an old atmosphere, which is proud of its noble past as a duchy. Its many precious monuments include the Cathedral and Baptistery (left) and Piazza Garibaldi, with the Palazzo del Governo and Clock Tower (bottom right).

225
Emilia Romagna –
REGGIO EMILIA

Reggio Emilia is a dynamic, modern city that has preserved the medieval layout of its historic district, which was embellished by the Este rulers during the Renaissance. The heart of the city is Piazza Prampolini (left), which the city's inhabitants have always referred to as "Piazza Grande". This square is lined with the buildings that symbolize city life: the Cathedral with its Romanesque Baptistery and the Town Hall.

226-227
Emilia Romagna – BOLOGNA

Bologna is variously referred to as "fat", due to its culinary traditions, "learned" for its university and "turreted" for the towers and campanili that dominate the city. The two most famous towers of the nobility (center) are the 325-foot Asinelli Tower and the 165-foot Garisenda Tower. Both overlook the Piazza di Porta Ravegnana that captures the charm of the oldest part of Bologna, together with Piazza Maggiore and Piazza del Nettuno.

228
Tuscany – FLORENCE

Florence is a sublime city, which combines the enchantment of art with the prestige of history, interweaving them to form a lively urban fabric. Its beauty and evocative capacity are unrivalled throughout the world. The 14th-century Ponte Vecchio is one of the symbols of the city. It is lined with 16th-century shops and characterized by an elevated walkway, the Vasari Corridor, which connects the Uffizi to the Pitti Palace.

229
Tuscany – FLORENCE

The Arno runs through Florence from east to west and is crossed by numerous monumental bridges that resisted the 1966 flood. Its banks are lined with an alternating series of medieval houses and palaces, which were flooded during the dramatic inundation, but have now been restored to their old splendor.

230-231
Tuscany – FLORENCE

The Medici city center of Florence is concentrated to the north of the Arno and has two focuses: the religious nucleus formed by Santa Maria del Fiore, the Baptistery and Giotto's Campanile (left) and the civic nucleus, formed by Piazza della Signoria, Palazzo Vecchio, the Uffizi and Ponte Vecchio (center). Beyond the river it is possible to discern the Pitti Palace and the fringes of the Boboli Gardens (bottom, right).

232-233
Tuscany – FLORENCE

The Cathedral of Santa Maria del Fiore is famous for its 350-foot high dome, built by Brunelleschi in 1434, and its delicate, slender campanile, designed by Giotto in 1334. It is a graceful marble jewel, begun by Arnolfo di Cambio in 1296, whose construction required over 130 years of work.

234
Tuscany – FLORENCE

Numerous pearls shine amidst the rooftops of Florence: the 13th-century Baptistery (top) that completes Piazza del Duomo; Santa Maria Novella (center), a fine example of Renaissance harmony; and the complex formed by the Uffizi, Piazza della Signoria and Palazzo Vecchio (bottom), which is the center of city life and site of a museum that attracts 1.5 million visitors each year.

235
Tuscany – FLORENCE

A splendid panorama of the entire city of Florence can be admired from the Certosa del Galluzzo (bottom). On the left it is possible to discern the walls of the Boboli Gardens, whilst the Cathedral's dome towers above the sea of houses (top).

236-237
Tuscany – FLORENCE

The 16th-century Italian-style Boboli Gardens extend south of the Pitti Palace. Designed by Brunelleschi and constructed in the 15th century, it now houses important art galleries and museums. The Church of Santo Spirito (1487) is visible on the left.

238

Tuscany – PISA

The Campo dei Miracoli is the monumental center of Pisa. During the age of the Maritime Republics the wealthy city state of Pisa decided to build a complex of magnificent buildings on this grassy area to bear witness to its prestige and power. The Pisan Romanesque-style Cathedral dates back to 1118 and its huge bulk is lightened and balanced by the 54 small marble columns that decorate its façade. A short path links it to the Baptistery, which was commenced in 1153 but not completed until 1400.

239

Tuscany – PISA

The Leaning Tower belongs to the Campo dei Miracoli complex of monumental buildings. It was constructed between the 12th and 14th centuries and is clad with white marble, encircled by six orders of columns. Part of its fame is due to its list, which was caused by the subsidence of the underlying ground over the centuries.

240-241

Tuscany – PISA

Pisa's medieval historic district is concentrated around the Arno (right), while the Campo dei Miracoli stands directly to the north. This complex is also home to the 13th-century Camposanto (left), built within the old city walls (bottom).

242 | **Tuscany – LIVORNO** | Piazza della Repubblica, formerly known as Piazza Carlo Alberto, was bombarded during World War II and subsequently rebuilt. It stands in the historic district of the Tuscan city near the port, which is the nerve center and commercial hub of the entire region.

243 | **Tuscany – LUCCA** | The Church of San Michele was built in the 12th century on the site of the ancient Roman forum, explaining why it is also known as San Michele in Foro. The elegant square next to the church is lined with famous palaces, such as the Palazzo Pretorio, and the house where Giacomo Puccini was born, which now houses a museum dedicated to the composer.

244-245 | **Tuscany – LUCCA** | Piazza del Mercato is also known as Piazza Anfiteatro. The origin of this name is clear from its oval shape, for the houses that line the square were built along the walls of the Roman amphitheater constructed in the 2nd century AD.

246 | Siena owes its beauty to a particular blend of history, art and natural charms. The majestic city is enclosed by medieval walls and
Tuscany – SIENA | stands atop a rise in the heart of Italy's most beautiful and famous hills. City life revolves around the two main squares, the Campo and Piazza del Duomo, but is constantly fueled by the rivalry of the 17 wards of the city – contrade – that is vented twice a year in the Palio.

247 | The Cathedral is a masterpiece of late-
Tuscany – SIENA | medieval Tuscan art and was inspired by the Romanesque-Gothic style. It was commenced during the second half of the 12th century and completed in the 14th century. The richly-decorated polychrome marble façade is largely the work of Giovanni Pisano.

248-249
Tuscany — SIENA

The Palazzo Pubblico dates back to the early 14th century. The Gothic-style building is dominated by the 290-foot medieval Mangia Tower, which rises above the 15th-century chapel built at its base as a votive offering following the Black Death of 1348.

248
Tuscany — SIENA

Piazza del Campo offers an evocative view of an extraordinary monumental complex and a daring geometric layout. The shell-shaped square slopes gently down towards the Palazzo Pubblico and is the setting for the biannual Palio horse race.

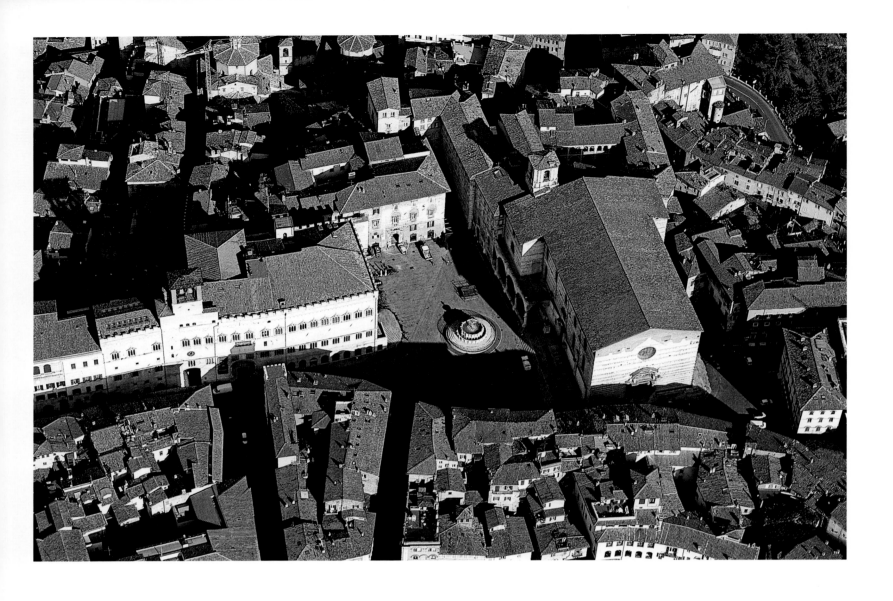

250 | Piazza IV Novembre is the heart of the old city and is lined with the most famous monuments of the age
Umbria – PERUGIA | of the Communes, from the Palazzo dei Priori to the Cathedral. The Fontana Maggiore stands in the
middle of the square. This fountain was built in 1278 and decorated with sculptures by Niccolò and
Giovanni Pisano.

251 | Urbino clings to the high ground that overlooks the gentle Marchigian hills and is dominated by the Ducal Palace (the
Marche – URBINO | rectangular building top left). Still enclosed by its medieval walls, the city is scattered with many buildings from the 15th-
century, the period in which it reached the height of its splendor under the rule of the Montefeltro family.

254-255

Lazio – ROME The Tiber caresses the heart of Rome, crossed by monumental bridges. Castel Sant'Angelo is visible on the left. This former imperial mausoleum, fortress and symbol of papal power is now a museum. The 16th-century district, composed of densely packed streets that open onto unexpected flower-adorned squares, can be seen in the center. The huge white shape of the Vittoriano, a monument erected in honor of King Vittorio Emanuele II, is visible in the distance.

256
Lazio – ROME
The Fountain of Neptune occupies the northern focus of elliptical Piazza Navona. It was remodeled by Bernini and the current statuary group (sea horses, mermaids and cherubs playing with dolphins) was added in the 19th century.

257
Lazio – ROME
Piazza Navona stands on the site of the ancient Stadium of Domitian, whose shape it follows. The Fountain of the Four Rivers, completed in 1651 by Bernini, stands at its center. The Fountain of Neptune is situated on the northern side and the Fountain of the Moor on the southern side.

258 | Piazza del Popolo is one of Rome's largest squares and was built at the beginning of the 19th century
Lazio – ROME | by Giuseppe Valadier. It links Via del Corso (top, announced by two Baroque churches) with the Pincio
Terrace (left) and takes its name from the old Porta del Popolo (bottom left).

259 | Piazza di Spagna owes its name to the Spanish embassy, which occupied a nearby palace in the 17th century.
Lazio – ROME | Much of its charm is derived from the majestic Spanish Steps, which lead to the Trinità dei Monti Church and come
alive each evening with street artists and tourists seeking evocative sights.

The Trevi Fountain rises imposingly in the heart of Baroque Rome. This late 18th-century work by Nicola Salvi is one of the favorite destinations of visitors to the Eternal City, who are fascinated by the effects of light and water that bring the monument to life.

A long string of angels sculpted by Bernini accompanies those crossing Ponte Sant'Angelo, the bridge connecting the left bank of the Tiber to Castel Sant'Angelo. This imposing building was originally the mausoleum of the Emperor Hadrian and was subsequently transformed into a fortress and prison.

Rome is a huge archaeological park, where sites of great historical and artistic importance live side by side with the frenetic life of a great metropolis. The modern city in this photograph seems to besiege the remains of the Domus Augustana and Domus Flavia, which belonged to the imperial palace built by Domitian on the Palatine. The Forums (top left) and Colosseum (top right) can be seen in the distance.

264-265
Campania – NAPLES
Piazza del Plebiscito stands in the center of Naples and embodies the city's noble 19th-century soul. The rectangular part is closed by the Royal Palace, built at the beginning of the 17th century, while the semicircular section is bounded by the neoclassic Church of San Francesco di Paola, inspired by the Pantheon in Rome.

265 top
Campania – CASERTA
The Royal Palace at Caserta is considered the Neapolitan Versailles and was built in the 18th century by the famous architect Vanvitelli. The conception and proportions of the building are very grand, and it comprises 1,200 rooms – all sumptuously decorated – and extensive grounds, covering an area of around 250 acres.

265 center and bottom
Campania – NAPLES | Naples is a great city with an important history and boasts many buildings that testify to the fact. These include the Castel Nuovo (center), which recalls the centuries in which the city was home to the Angevin and Aragonese courts. However, Naples also offers splendid views over the bay dominated by Vesuvius, such as that which can be admired from the Port of Santa Lucia and Castel dell'Ovo (bottom).

266-267 | The center of Bari has maintained its popular and medieval appearance, composed of narrow streets and low houses. The

Apulia – BARI | Basilica of San Nicola, consecrated in 1197, stands at the center of the so-called Old City.

267
Apulia – LECCE

First Norman and then Angevin, for many centuries Lecce belonged to the Kingdom of Naples. At the height of the city's splendor several masterpieces were built in its historic district, earning it the name of "Baroque Florence".

268-269
Basilicata – MATERA

The Old City (bottom) stands at the foot of the New City and is an incredible mass of white houses overlapping each other. The Strada dei Sassi, with its evocative cave dwellings carved out of the rock, is a surprising sight.

270-271
Sicily – SYRACUSE | The ancient port and castle stand before Ortygia, the original and oldest nucleus of Syracuse. Greek colonists landed and founded a famous trading port on this splendid little island, connected to the mainland by a bridge.

271 top
Sicily – PALERMO | Palermo was founded by the Phoenicians and successively conquered by the Romans, followed by the Saracens. The Normans subsequently made it their capital, transforming an old Arab fortress into a palace– now known as the Norman Palace – and political and administrative headquarters.

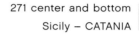

271 center and bottom
Sicily – CATANIA

Catania is Sicily's second-largest city and is dominated by the presence of Etna. It was almost completely destroyed by an earthquake in 1693, but its historic district nonetheless preserves little jewels of Baroque architecture, such as the Cathedral (center).

272-273
Sicily – RAGUSA

The orderly higher city of Ragusa, with its "modern" plan, dates back to the 18th century, when it was built to fill the empty areas left by the earthquake of 1693, which had devastated the lower city.

272
Sicily – RAGUSA

Ragusa has very ancient origins and was the stronghold of the Siculi, who retreated to the interior to escape the colonization of the coasts. Modern Ragusa has a dual identity, due to the ingenious and complicated system of stairs that connect the old city to the new one.

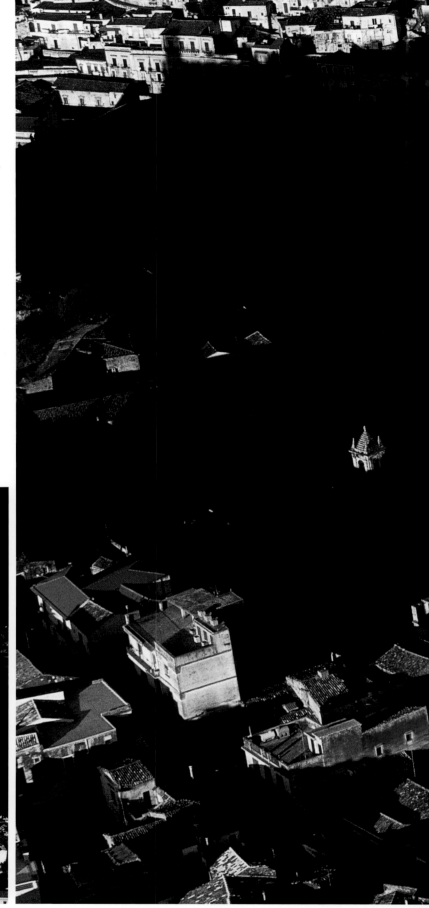

274-275
Sardinia – CAGLIARI | Cagliari was a crucial node in the network of Mediterranean trading routes. The city's oldest monuments include the Castle, the Cathedral and the Church of the Purissima, although modern life is concentrated in the area around the port (in the foreground).

Cagliari is situated in an enviable position amid beaches, hills and inland lagoons. Its pool and saltpans offer refuge to a huge range of birds, including many flamingoes.

ROLLING HILLS, GREEN PLAINS

Italy's hills and plains betray centuries of close relations with man, his work and his settlements. A farmstead or a village is a fitting complement to both rolling and severe countryscapes, in which the hand of man is nonetheless always visible.

ROLLING HILLS, GREEN PLAINS

HORIZONS

The hilly land of the Orcia Valley, where the main crops are cereals and legumes, is delimited by clearings and dirt tracks, known as "white roads", shaded by the slender silhouettes of cypress trees.

Valleys, hills, plains, lakes, rivers and forests: lowland Italy is an extraordinary mosaic of shapes and colors that fit together like brushstrokes of a great fresco, magically forming a perfectly proportioned picture when viewed from the air. The forests are an inviting green carpet, the plains and hills a patchwork blanket, the rivers are arteries carrying an iridescent, silvery lifeblood and the lakes small fragments of sky hidden amid the vegetation. In Italy nature is not only white glaciers, the pink Dolomites, blue sea and green islands, for the land whose frontiers are bounded by the Alpine peaks and Mediterranean coasts is extremely fragmented and thus very diverse. Not far from the great plain created by the Po, whose landscape is shaped by alternating fields and towns, lie extensive hilly areas. These are dotted with fewer, irregularly spaced vineyards and fields of wheat and sunflowers, mixed with woods, recalling the times in which the low hills were the home of deer and wild boar. On the edges of the plains, where the lowlands give way to the mountains, numerous prealpine lakes collect the water of the rivers and mountain streams. Toward the south the landscapes take on an arid beauty: the desolate valleys of the torrents of southern continental Italy – sun-scorched and windblown lands – the granite highlands of northwestern Sardinia and the ravines of Apulia. These landscapes with their own vegetation, sky and light are actually far nearer than we might assume from their diversity. The woodlands, Italy's ancient green lungs, have survived at high altitudes; only scattered and often ailing oases remain beneath 2,500 feet, often following the courses of rivers. Wounded by man, the forests paradoxically owe their survival to

284-285
Piedmont – LANGHE | The rural landscape of the Langhe is defined by a lively and variegated patchwork of irregular glades of poplars, fields ready for sowing or harvesting and vineyards crossed by the snaking silver ribbon of the Tanaro.

284
Piedmont - LANGHE | The last snowy traces of winter linger before giving way to spring around this farm in the Langhe near Castelletto Stura, in the province of Cuneo.

286-287 | The Langhe hills are ideal for winegrowing. The finest Piedmontese wines are obtained from
Piedmont - LANGHE | grapes grown on the *bric*, the upper part of the hill, in the sunniest position.

288-289 and 290-291 | The appearance of the paddy fields of the Vercelli area – in this case close to Palazzolo – varies according to season.
Piedmont – VERCELLI AREA | In winter they are expanses of ice and snow that look like an extension of Monte Rosa, in spring mirrors that reflect the
sky, and in summer colored patches – first green, turning to ocher in September.

292
**LAKE GARDA, LAKE COMO
AND LAKE MAGGIORE** | The landscape of the foothills of the Alps, stretching from Piedmont to Veneto, is dotted with lakes, whose shores and islands are home to testimonials of the past and spectacular natural corners. The highlights include Lake Garda with the Scaligeri Castle in Sirmione (top), Lake Como with the Bellagio promontory (bottom left) and Lake Maggiore with Isola Bella and the Borromeo Palace (bottom right).

**292 bottom center and 293
Piedmont – LAKE ORTA** | The island of San Giulio, a jewel emerging from the waters of Lake Orta, takes its name from the saint who evangelized the area in the 4th century AD. It is home to an early Christian basilica, purported to have been founded by the saint in 390, and an enclosed convent.

294-295
Piedmont – LAKE MAGGIORE | Isola Bella, on Lake Maggiore, is almost completely occupied by the Baroque palace built in the 17th century by Count Vitaliano Borromeo. The building is set in elegant Italian-style gardens.

294
Piedmont – LAKE MAGGIORE | Isola dei Pescatori has maintained its original layout of an old village crossed by winding alleys and dominated by the Church and Campanile of San Vittore.

296-297 | The Po is subject to a geological phenomenon known as resurgence. When rainwater and the waters of the river encounter
Piedmont – PO RIVER | permeable soil, they are absorbed and do not resurface until they reach the impermeable strata of the lower valley.

298-299 | The Tagliamento, which rises on Monte Miaron and flows into the Adriatic Sea, broadens near the Veneto coast until
Friuli Venezia Giulia – TAGLIAMENTO RIVER | reaching an average width of 3,000 feet and assuming the typical conformation of interlacing canals.

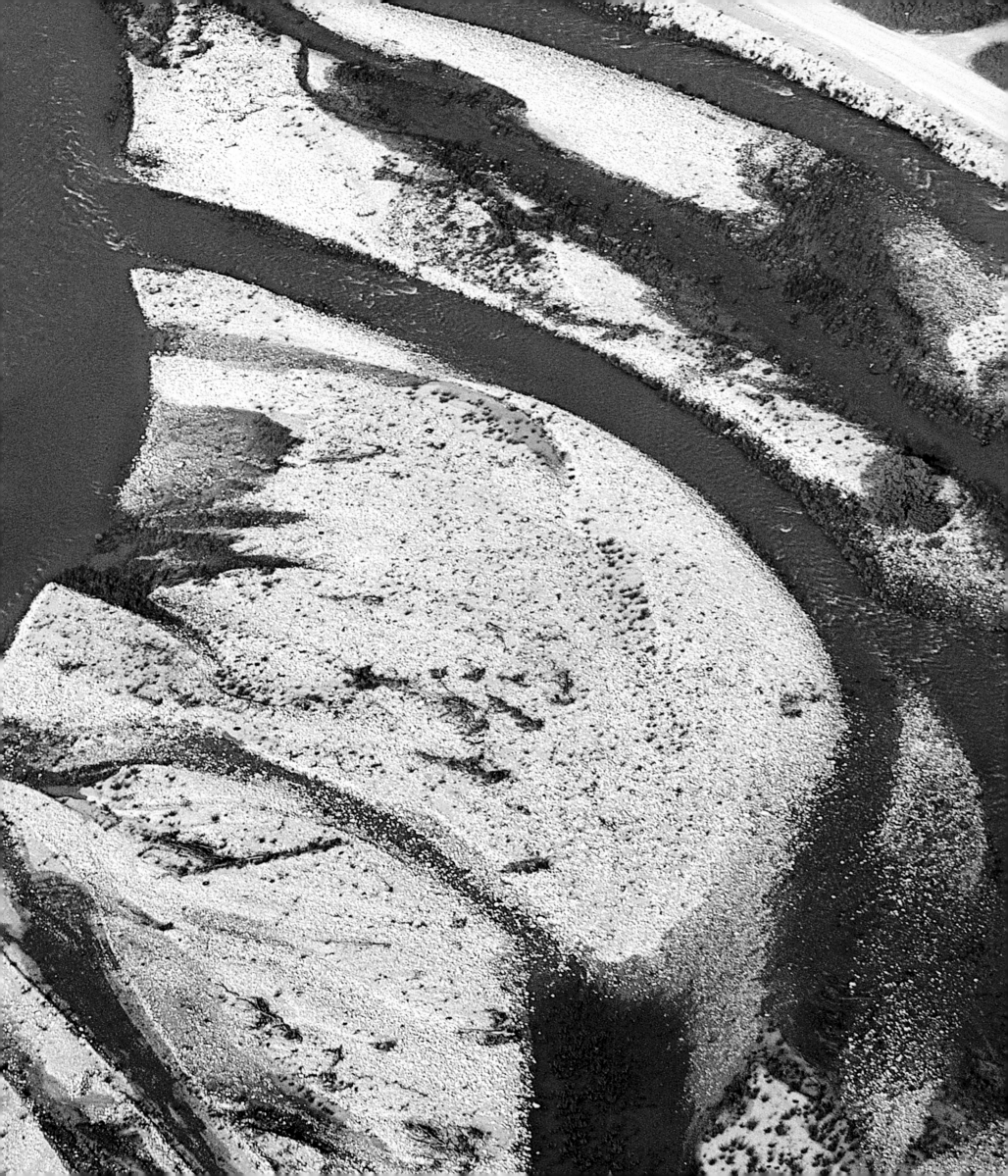

300 | Veneto – LAGOON | The Venice Lagoon is composed of shallow expanses of natural or artificial saltwater. These are ideal for fish farming, with their embankments, channels, collection and overwintering pools, fresh and saltwater inlets and *chiaviche*, the typical sluice gates that allow the passage of the fish.

301 | Veneto – POLESINE | After having crossed four regions (Piedmont, Lombardy, Emilia Romagna and Veneto), the Po flows into the Adriatic Sea, forming a wide delta that radiates into a web of channels reaching out in many directions in the lower Polesine.

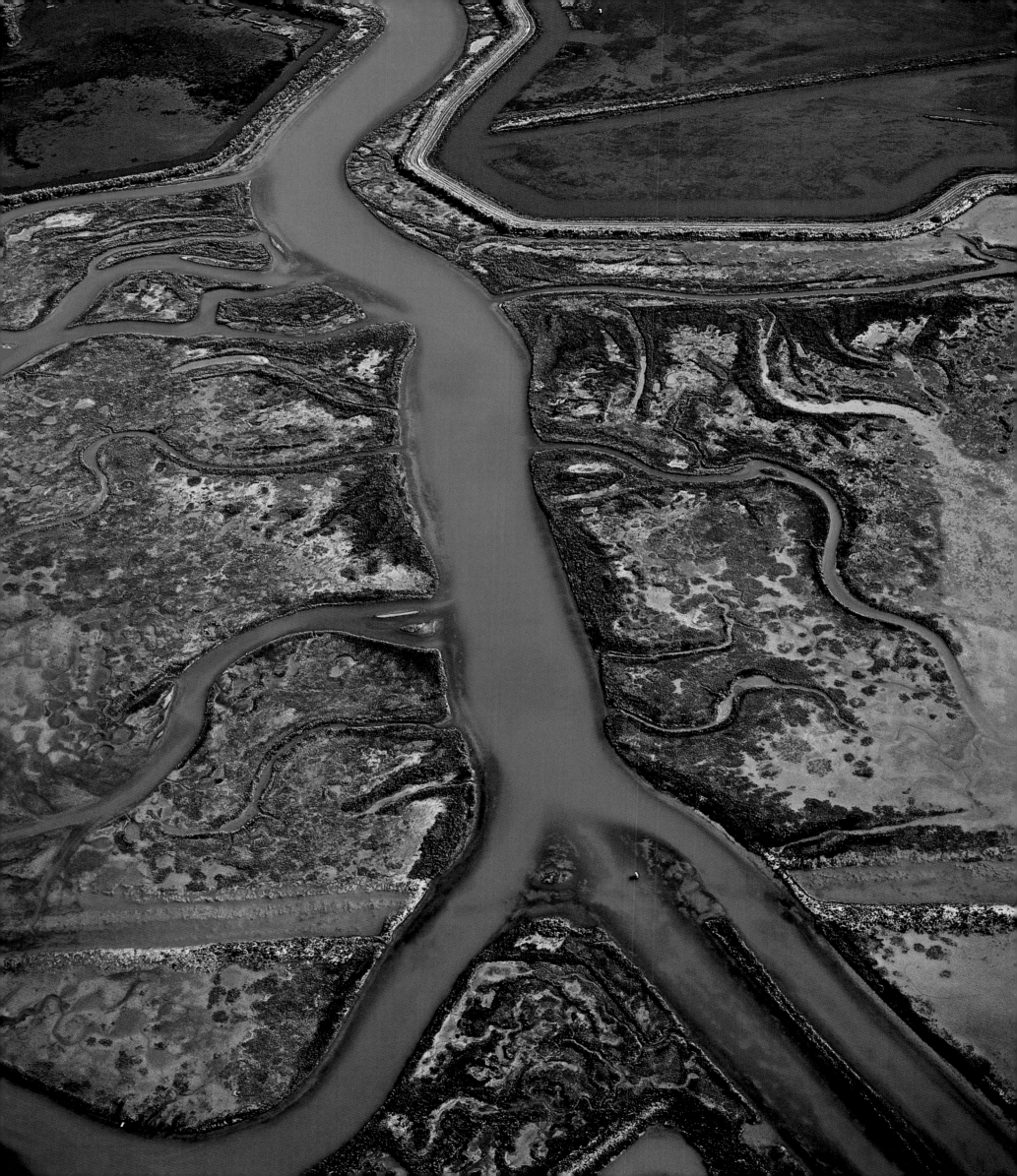

302 and 303 | During the spring and summer, the high ground of the Emilian Apennines – shown here in the area
Emilia-Romagna – EMILIAN APENNINES | around Carpineti, in the province of Emilia Romagna – is often swathed in a blanket of morning mist,
hiding the meadows, houses and woods.

304-305 | The colors of the rural houses recall those of the plowed fields and are scattered over the predominantly green
Emilia-Romagna – EMILIAN APENNINES | Apennine landscape characterized by luxuriant woods and numerous meadows.

306-307 | At low altitudes the meadows and cultivated fields leave little space for woods. However, woodland occupies most of the
Emilia-Romagna – EMILIAN APENNINES | mountain slopes above 2,600 feet.

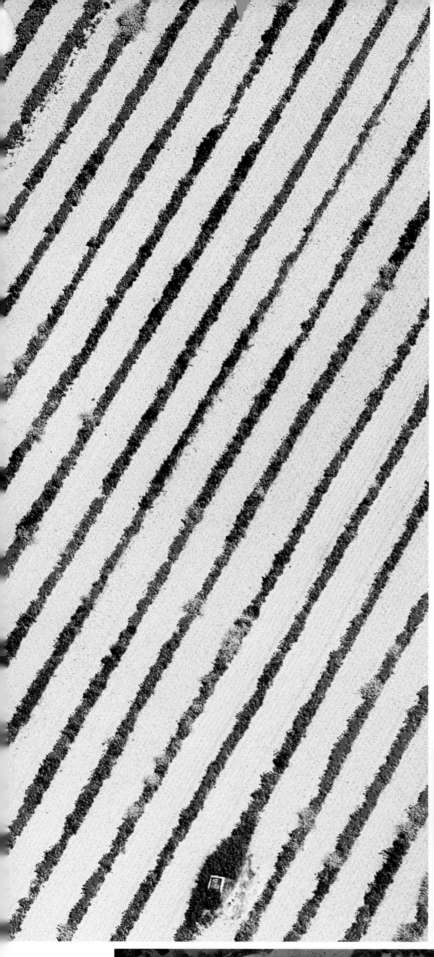

The Po River Valley makes Emilia Romagna Italy's most productive region. The most widely grown crops of the farmland around Reggio Emilia – and many other areas of Emilia – are cereals, fruit and vegetables. Seen from above, the colors and symmetrical patterns of the cultivated areas form striking and sometimes deceiving effects.

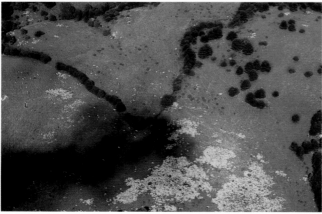

310-311
Tuscany – CHIANTI The Tuscan countryside is dotted with farmsteads at the center of small plots of cultivated land – a legacy of the times in which the sharecropping system was used for farming.

311
Tuscany – SIENA AREA The areas planted with cereals and furrowed by the passage of farm machinery, near Monteriggioni, are broken by areas of woodland that often mark the boundaries of the properties.

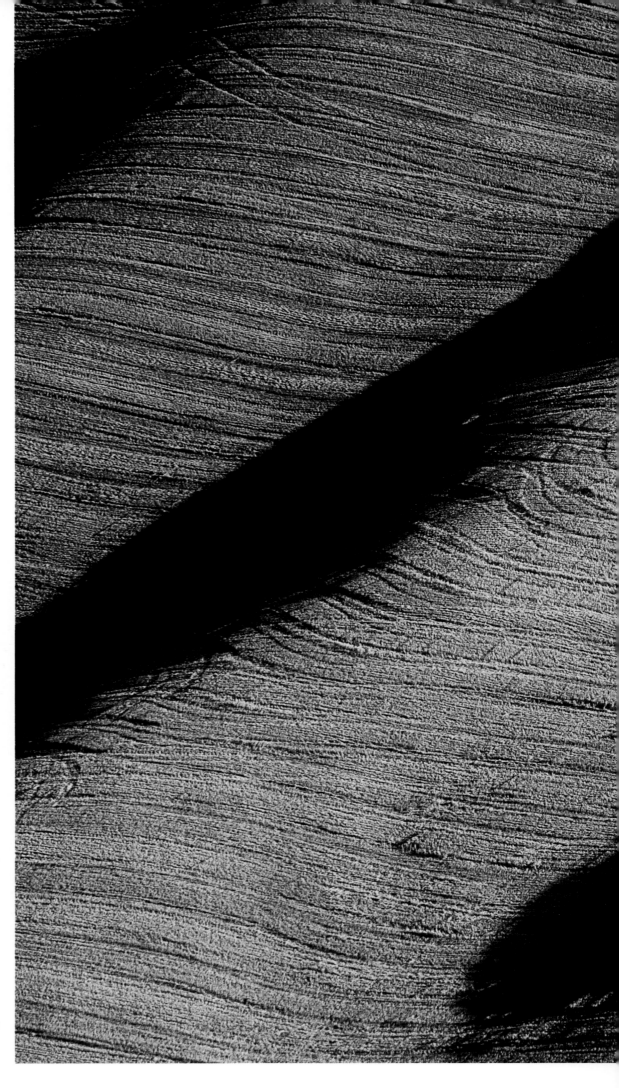

312-313
Tuscany – CRETE SENESI | In summer, the freshly plowed fields of the clay hills of the countryside around Siena resemble velvet patches. At certain times of day the sunlight sets them ablaze with hues of deep ocher yellow.

314-315
Tuscany – PRATO | Orderly geometric fields surround an isolated farmstead in the countryside around Prato. The tall cypress trees lining the approach to the farm are typical of this area and central Italy in general.

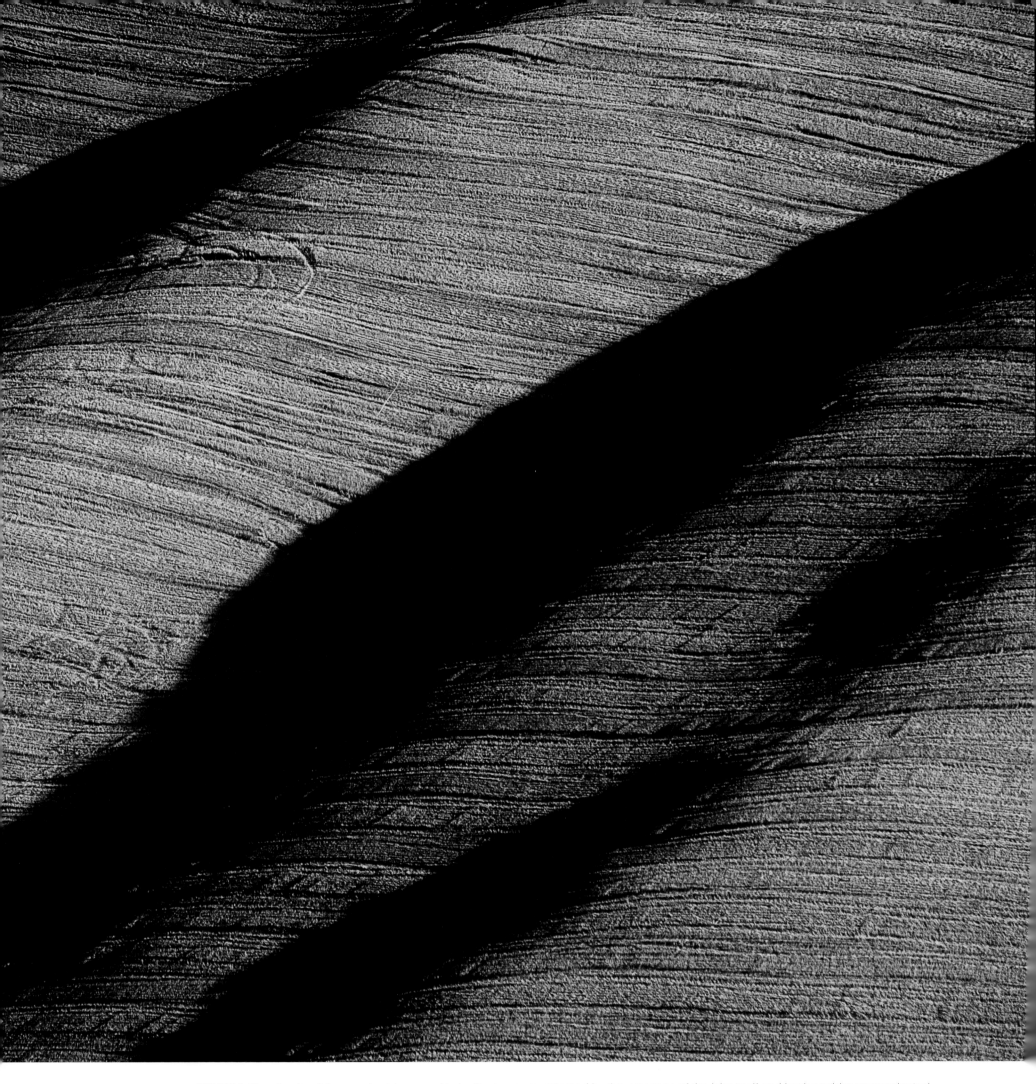

316-317

Umbria

The climate of the countryside around Lake Trasimeno is mitigated by the presence of the lake itself and by the milder meteorological conditions of the western part of the region of Umbria, making it suitable for the cultivation of vines, olives and certain kinds of legumes.

318-319
Marche The flat areas of the Marche region are situated along the coast, while the rest of the territory is mainly hilly and mountainous. They are used for growing wheat, fruit, olives, sugar beet and grapes for winemaking.

320 and 321
Umbria – LAKE TRASIMENO

The shores of Lake Trasimeno are home to historical buildings (left) as well as the archaeological sites of famous battles, and are set against a lush green backdrop. Isola Minore (right), one of the lake's three islands, also has a long history. It was inhabited up until the 15th century and only abandoned following frequent raids by bandits.

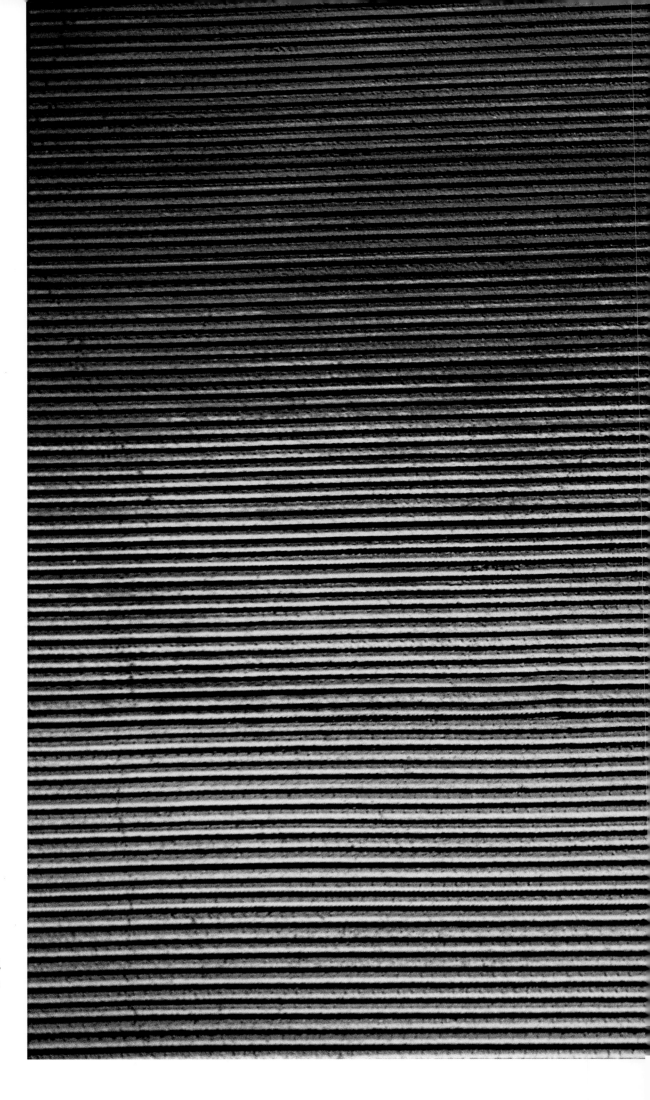

322-323
Lazio – MOUNT CIRCEO
Seen from above, this plowed land near the Circeo National Park closely resembles a work of modern or abstract art.

324-325
Campania – SALERNO AREA
Campania's plains are very fertile, due to their volcanic soil, and are ideal for the cultivation of many kinds of fruit and vegetable, both in fields and under glass, according to the season and type of produce.

326-327 | The conifer woods of southern Italy, such as this one between Salerno and Paestum, are chiefly
Campania – SALERNO AREA | constituted by maritime pines, with their unmistakable umbrella-like shape.

328-329
Apulia – CASTEL DEL MONTE

The huge octagonal form of Castel del Monte, which many scholars believe to be an architectural representation of esoteric principles, dominates one of the highest hills of the Western Murgia, south of Andria, in Apulia.

328
Apulia – CASTEL DEL MONTE

The castle was built by Frederick II of Swabia – the grandson of Frederick I Barbarossa, Holy Roman Emperor and King of Sicily – in the middle of the 13th century. It was not designed as a military fortress, for it has no defensive architectural features.

330
Sicily – RAGUSA COUNTRYSIDE

The land around Ragusa is baked by the sun, but nonetheless farmed or used for grazing after having been claimed from the mountain and rocks by the work of generations of peasants. Solitary *masserie* can be seen between the cereal fields. These limestone buildings, which blend well with the surrounding landscape, were once associated with livestock farming and other agricultural activities.

331
Sicily – SLOPES OF ETNA

On the slopes of Mount Etna, which rises almost 11,000 feet, an abandoned farm in an area hit by a violent eruption looks as though it is about to be swallowed up by the surrounding lava, which encircles it with an unbroken black expanse as far as the eye can see. Indeed, the landscape above 10,000 feet is dominated by a volcanic desert, which leaves no room for plant life.

332-333
Sardinia – ORISTANO

The wetlands of the upper part of the Sinis Peninsula, near Oristano, are composed of brackish and freshwater pools, lagoons and lakes. This natural oasis is home to pink flamingoes (in the photograph), as well as various other species of birds, some of which are permanent residents, like cormorants and herons, and other seasonal visitors, such as wild geese and grebes.

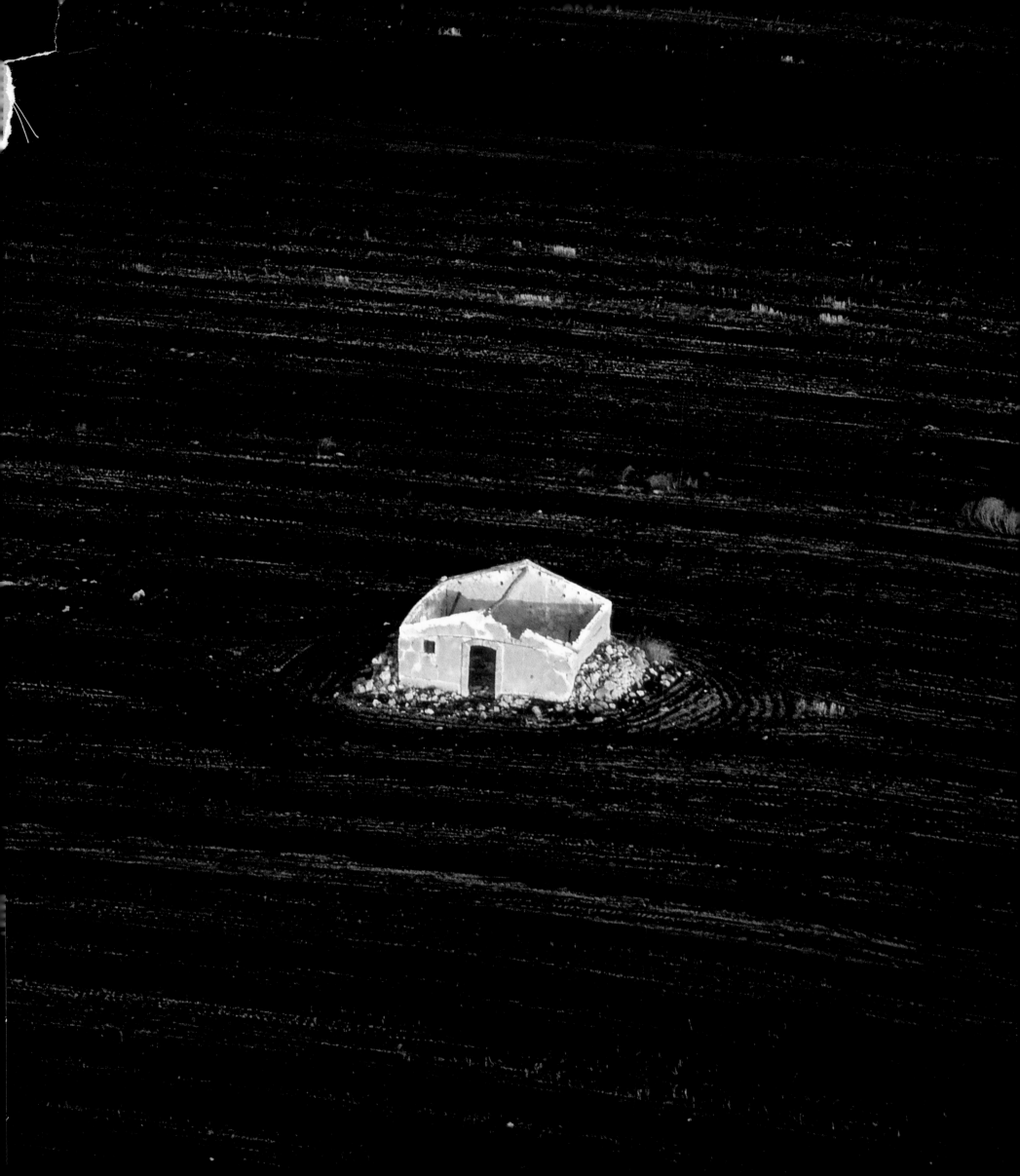

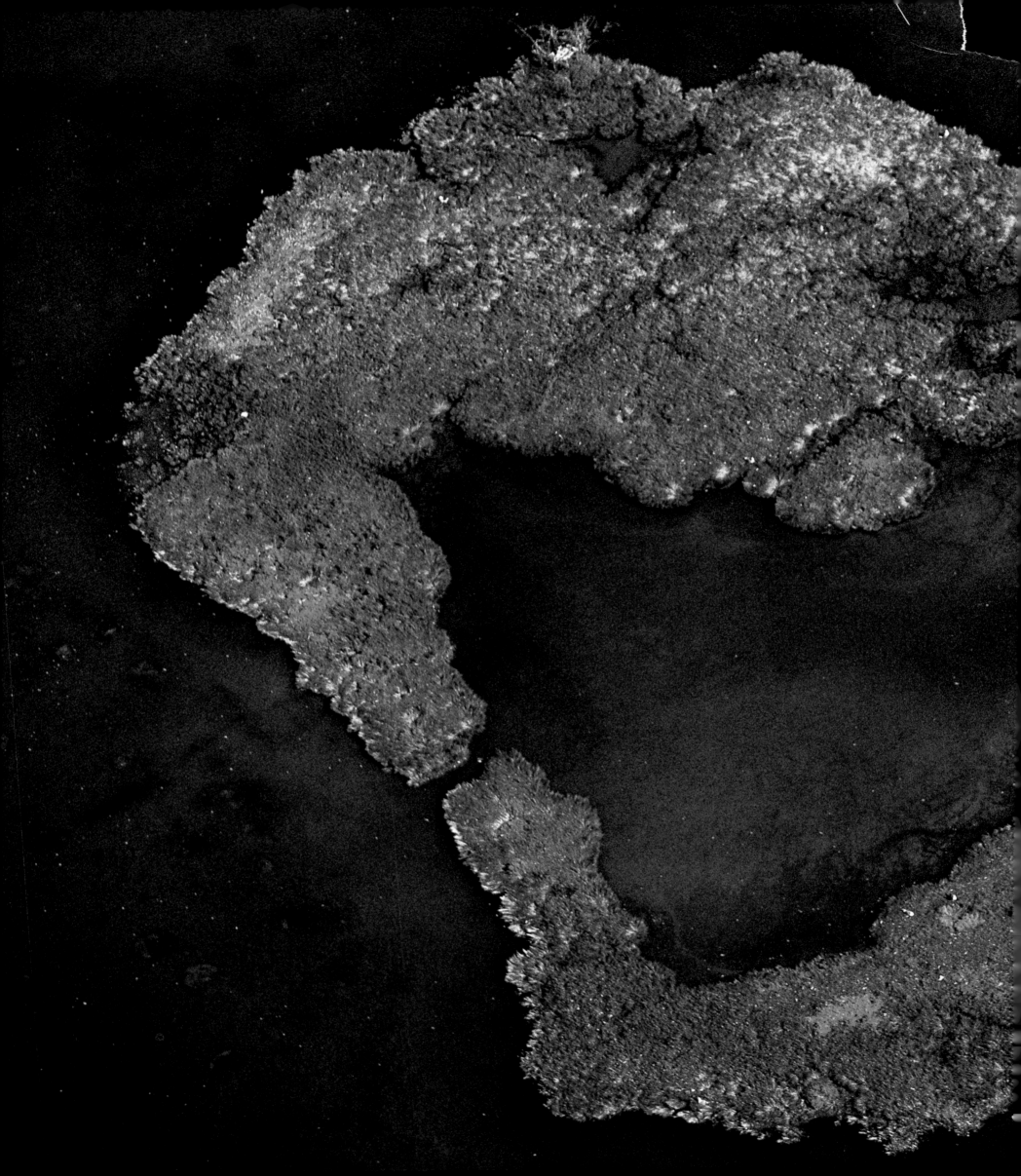

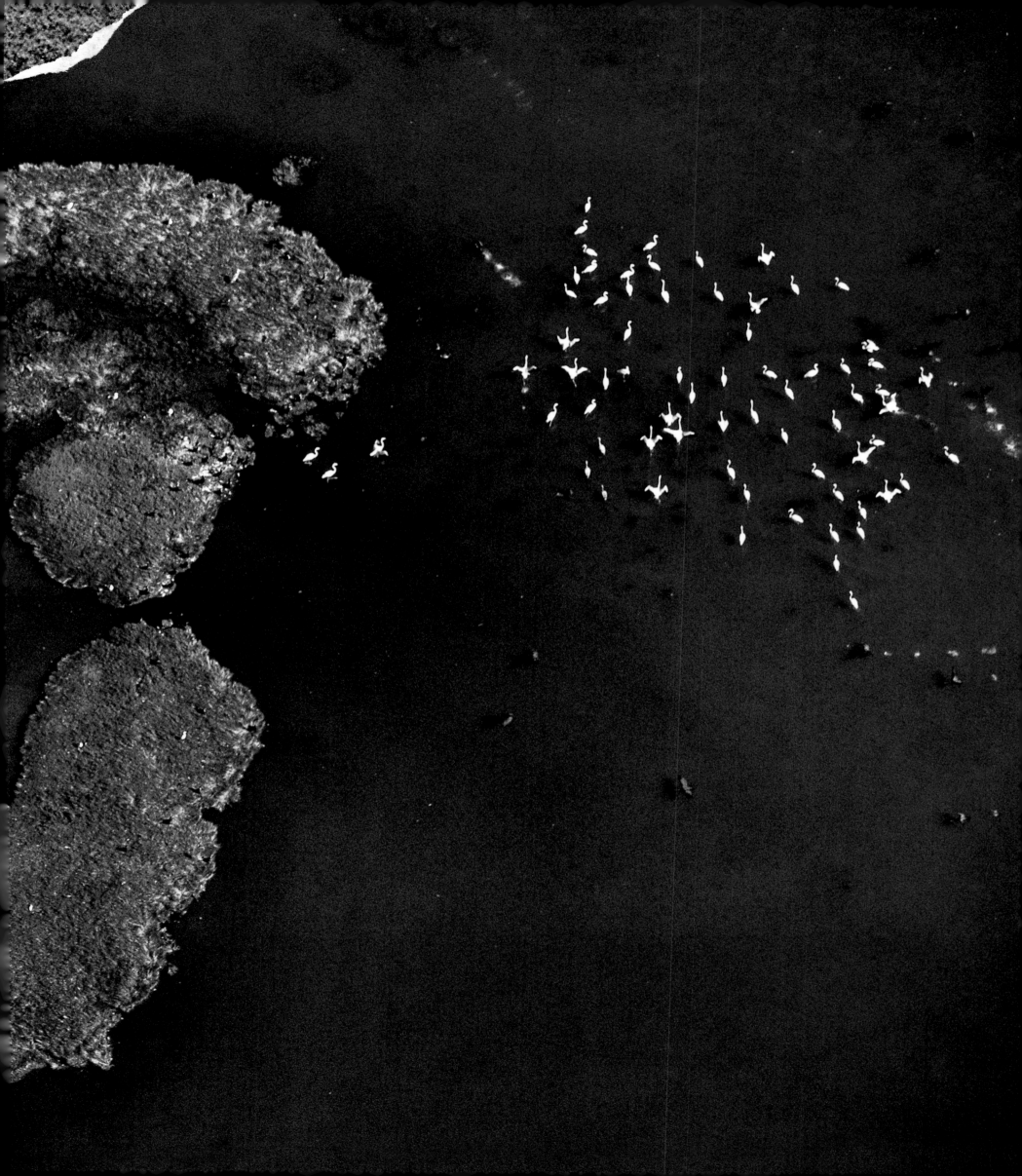

TOWNS AND VILLAGES

Italy's great variety of historic districts, castles, hamlets, towns and villages on the plains, hillsides, riverbanks and coasts represent a great artistic and historical wealth. Much of the modern country is directly descended from that world, which developed in the unstable but very fertile equilibrium, of the many city-states.

LITTLE GEMS

Gallipoli is located on the western coast of the Salentine Peninsula. Its evocative historic district, with its many old white buildings, stands on a limestone island that is connected to the mainland by a masonry bridge. The photograph shows a section of the old walls and, above, the island of Sant'Andrea, which is home to a great lighthouse, built in 1866.

"The sky ends a few feet above, amid yellow fumes, the pillars of overpasses, hanging washing, power lines and suspended oily soot. All around is a seemingly inextricable roaring and screaming world, yet there is still room for the cricket, the half-eaten apple, the child and the motionless eye of the goat." This is how Carlo Levi described the modern village: a place that recounts the old and the new, man and nature, progress, pollution and the rhythms of town and country. He drew a true a portrait of the small towns and villages, which are just as important for driving everyday life as the greatest cities. The old village, nestling inside the new one, is often perched atop the highest hill. It allows us to follow and identify the traces of the times and civic and religious history of the people who inhabited them, or simply lose ourselves in their inextricable maze of narrow streets. The old nucleus, enclosed and fortified by walls, spreads out over spacious terraces, which resemble balconies offering enchanting views.

We encountered these breathtakingly beautiful villages during our flight: seen from above, the small and numerous urban settlements that dot the peninsula, from Monteriggioni, Montepulciano and Assisi to Gubbio, Asolo and Bassano del Grappa, are jewels set in velvet country landscapes, each with its own peculiar shape and facets. Circular walled towns declaring their medieval origins rest on gentle hills, like nests in trees; chaotic agglomerations reveal the overlap of different periods; small chains of colored houses stretching along the coast recall continuous adaptations to the lay of the land; and towers and belfries demonstrate a rich history and lively contrasts between temporal and religious power.

Italy has a thousand identities, one for each inhabited settlement, down to the tiniest village. Wars, invasions, blood and pain have glorified the role of the small towns. Great works of engineering and masterpieces of art and architecture were built to serve this yearning and ensure the survival of the community. Italian feudal and agricultural society was based on the self-sufficiency of the built-up areas.

Everything began with castles that are, after all, nuclei of small towns. Today they emanate the allure of fortified architecture, with soaring towers, crenellated walls, buttresses and communication trenches, all of which can all be seen from above at a single glance. Within the walls it is possible to make out the residence of the lord and knights, the presbytery and the artisans' homes. Farther out, the ring of new walls encloses the red roofs of other houses. As in a journey through time, the fortified village gradually materializes, in some cases becoming a walled city and in others a majestic fortress. In Veneto, Tuscany and Umbria the plans and elegant palaces of many towns and villages reflect their old opulence, which permitted the emergence of the merchant middle class and banking, which invested resources in technological innovation and acted as a stimulus to art. Each of these settlements has lived through moments of splendor and decline, following the cycles of history, as indelibly testified by their physiognomies. History

placed the Italian villages at the center of the life of the entire country: they are simultaneously the warp and weft of the fabric and the embroidery that embellishes it; the background of a splendid portrait and the subject that enlivens it; the towers that enhance the profile of a hill, the piazza that encapsulates the dreams of the men who inhabit it and the palaces that legitimize its pride.

Flying on the wings of a bird, the small towns, castles and villages appear without any secrets. The traces left by time are clearly visible from the sky, like a chart or, better still, a portrait: every single wrinkle, expression and imperfection corresponds to a historical wound, a maneuver or an event in the past of the settlements' communities. Thus, the southern seaports still reflect their Hellenic nobility, while an indelible mark is impressed on the villages of Roman origin, with their typical square plans, and on the numerous satellites of Rome. Similarly, history has determined the location and structure of the villages along the Lazio coast and in Campania and the small towns that developed along the main roads that radiated out from the capital. Everywhere, the events of the past arouse the evocative sensations of the present. During the time of the decline of the Roman Empire and the ensuing barbarian invasions, numerous fortified villages founded on the high ground were protected by a ring of wall-houses. The original nuclei of Lucignano, Città del Pieve and Monte San Savino date back to this historical period. Authentic rings of walls interspersed with towers were built around these same villages during the Middle Ages. San Gimignano, the quintessential multi-towered village, recalls the period in which noble families ruled the towns, determining their appearances. In the maritime villages, on the other hand, the first private palaces were built by wealthy merchants, and several simple fishermen's villages with closely-packed houses and small evil-smelling squares developed into small ports displaying the luster that derives from art and architecture. Many fascinating examples of these can be found from Liguria to the upper reaches of the Adriatic and from the Sorrento coast to Sicily. Local geography naturally played an important role and explains the morphology of the towns and villages of the Campanian coast, from Amalfi to Sorrento, with their terraced, overlapping layout with disorderly vertical houses, clearly visible in our aerial pictures. It also underlies the series of characteristic narrow alleys known as *carruggi* that converge towards the port in all the Ligurian villages– from Portofino, Sestri Levante and Camogli to the Cinque Terre wedged between a narrow strip of coast and the Apennines; the close network of alleys of the island villages, from Murano and Burano to Orta San Giulio; and the hill towns of southern Italy, such as Alberobello and Ostuni. However, whether whitewashed or red-bricked, reflected in the blue sea or surrounded by the green hills, all the villages scattered over the peninsula share one characteristic: the piazza, which is the fulcrum and heart of civic life, an emblem and a rendezvous. Our journey through the Italian skies is populated by squares of all shapes and "ambitions": grand, with steps that emphasize the importance of monuments, such as that of Todi; interlocking, like San Gimignano's Piazza della Cisterna, Piazza del Duomo and Piazza delle Erbe; or terraced, overlooking the sea, as in many coastal towns, from Cervo to Cefalù.

Today it is easier than ever to read the history of cities in that of small towns and villages: some, like seeds that have never completely germinated, possess the genetic makeup of cities on a smaller scale, while others are complete municipalities that have used their compact dimensions to reach an ideal equilibrium with their surrounding environment and the needs of their inhabitants. They are artistic gems in which it is still a pleasure to live and which modestly offer their intrinsic beauty to our keen gaze.

340
Valle d'Aosta | Castles played in important role in the development of towns. In medieval times villages often grew up around fortresses and, over the centuries, developed into the nuclei of towns. The photographs show some of the famous castles that overlook the Valle d'Aosta. Fenis (top), Issogne (bottom left), Verres (bottom center) and Saint Pierre (bottom right).

341
Piedmont – FENESTRELLE | Seen from afar, the Fenestrelle fortifications appear as a long wall that climbs up the mountainside of the Chisone Valley from 3,725 to 3,840 feet. It is composed of 3 fortresses: Fort San Carlo, Fort Tre Denti and Fort delle Valli, which are connected by a staircase of almost 4,000 steps. Over 120 years were required to complete this gargantuan project, which is among the most impressive of the 18th century.

342-343
Piedmont – COSTIGLIOLE D'ASTI

Piedmontese towns are often situated on hilltops and dominated by manors. One of these is Costigliole d'Asti, between the Tanaro and Tinella valleys. Its name is derived from *Costigliolis*, a diminutive of "hillside", in reference to its high position. The castle was built in the 14th and 15th centuries, although its current appearance dates back to the 19th century, when it was extensively remodeled.

343
Piedmont – BAROLO

Piedmont's hill towns not only developed around castles, but also around churches. Those of the Langhe, for example, are built on hilltops or on two opposite hills. Barolo, renowned for its highly acclaimed and very fine wine, is a good example of this kind of town.

344-345
Piedmont – MONFERRATO

Monferrato is a geological neighbor of the Langhe and was one of the most organized "sub-nations" of northern Italy. This vaguely defined geographical entity has an unmistakable cultural identity, which can be seen at a glance in the layout of its small towns, derived from ancient fortifications.

346-347
Liguria – PORTOFINO

Portofino is a picturesque and internationally renowned fishing village of colored houses mirrored in the blue Ligurian Sea.

348-349
Liguria – CAMOGLI | Camogli has the characteristic colored houses typical of the Ligurian towns of the Riviera di Levante and is situated on the coast on the western edge of the Monte Portofino Natural Park. Its important maritime history earned it the name of "the town of the thousand white sailing ships". The photograph shows the old port and Dragonara Castle (left), built on a rocky headland next to the Church of Santa Maria Assunta (bottom center).

 349

Liguria

Liguria's coast is dotted with little towns as a result of both the region's history and geological morphology. Each of these has its own particular features and charm, like Sestri Levante, magically strewn along a peninsula, or Rapallo, set in a sea of oleanders and camellias (center). A faint thread connects the Ligurian towns, from east to west. This is the Aurelian Way (bottom, the stretch between Camogli and Recco), the old Roman road that snakes its way along the entire coast.

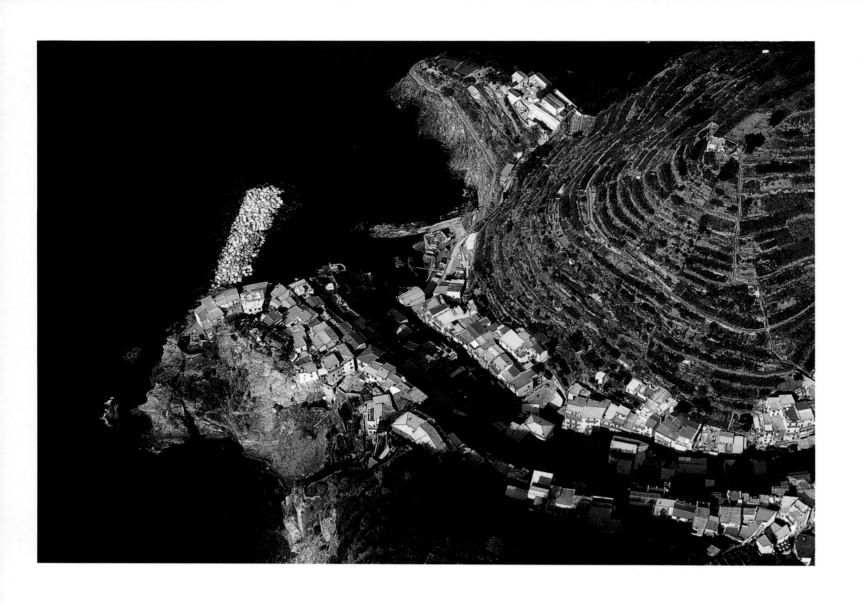

350 and 351
Liguria – CINQUE TERRE | The Cinque Terre are five small, characteristic towns situated in a breathtaking position between Levanto and Porto Venere. Their relatively inaccessible location, off the beaten tourist track, has enabled them to preserve their old appearance of maritime towns. The photographs show the easternmost of the five, Riomaggiore, whose center stands on a great rock dominated by a hill terraced with vineyards, which yield the grapes used for the local Sciacchetrà wine.

352 | The famous covered bridge of Bassano, destroyed during World War II and immediately rebuilt,
Veneto – BASSANO DEL GRAPPA | spans the Brenta River to connect the two parts of the town. It offers splendid views of the Altopiano
dei Sette Comuni and Monte Grappa.

353 | The harbor area of Bardolino, a tourist resort on Lake Garda, is renowned for its wine. Its historic district is embellished
Veneto – BARDOLINO | with churches and old towers and is surrounded by the remains of the walls erected by the della Scala rulers.

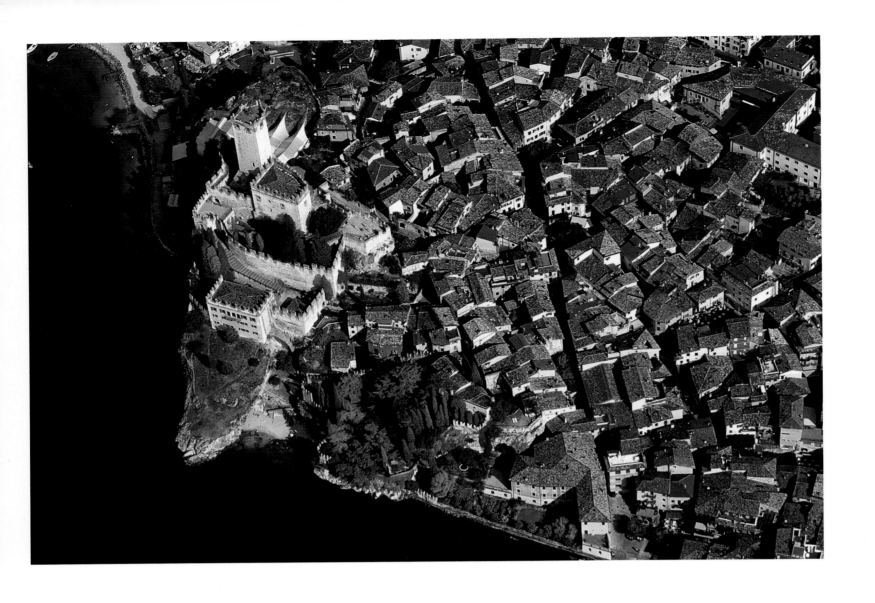

354 | Malcesine is an ancient town whose origins are lost in the mists of prehistory, but whose current structure
Veneto – MALCESINE | dates back to the early Middle Ages. It is dominated by a fortress that rises sheer above the waters of
Lake Garda. The Castle (left) was built by the Lombards during the same period (4th century AD).

355 | Asolo, still partly enclosed by late-Medieval walls, was disputed by Verona, Padua and Venice for many centuries,
Veneto – ASOLO | because of its strategic position. This photograph shows the town dominated by the fortress (top, far left), of pre-
Romanesque origin, but rebuilt between the end of the 12th and 13th century.

356-357 | Seen from above, the town of Burano in the Venice Lagoon is a patchwork of houses of a thousand colors, held together by a
Veneto – BURANO | web of canals plied by the typical flat-bottomed vessels. The façades are painted in a variety of pastel and saturated colors to
protect them from the corrosive sea air.

357
Veneto – VENICE LAGOON

In terms of landscape and biological variety, the Venice Lagoon is a wealth of beauty and poetry. Each island is a jewel: Murano (center) and Burano (top) look like little Venices, crisscrossed with canals and studded with picturesque old buildings. A legend relates that the Monastery of San Francesco del Deserto (bottom) marks the spot where Saint Francis landed on his return from the East in 1220.

358-359
Veneto – CHIOGGIA

The ancient maritime city of Chioggia lies at the southern tip of the Venice Lagoon. Like Venice itself, it is crossed by numerous navigable canals and a network of humpback bridges and is characterized by an aristocratic nucleus of elegant 16th and 17th-century Venetian-style houses. The 13th-century Monastery of San Domenico (top), located on a sandy island on the edge of the city, is one of Chioggia's finest monuments.

359
Emilia Romagna – COMACCHIO

Comacchio, a town built on the sand and water of the Po River Delta, is characterized by colorful fishermen's houses and canals crossed by curious short, wide bridges.

360-361
Emilia Romagna – SAN LEO
San Leo is a typical medieval hill-town on the slopes of the Emilian Apennines. It developed in a disorderly manner over the centuries, as shown by the irregular layout of its closely-packed houses.

361 bottom
Marche – OSTRA VETERE
The medieval walled town of Ostra Vetere, about 12 miles from Senigallia, in the province of Ancona, stands out against the green of the Marchigian hills, with the soaring steeple of its campanile and imposing dome of the Abbey of Santa Maria di Piazza.

361 top
Emilia Romagna A recent survey carried out in Emilia Romagna revealed the extraordinary number of castles, both medieval and medieval-style, situated in the region: at least 300 can still be seen today.

361 center
Emilia Romagna - TORRECHIARA Torrechiara Castle, built between 1448 and 1460 by nobleman Pier Maria Rossi, is situated in the municipality of Langhirano (Parma). It features fine grotesque decorations by Cesare Baglione. In recent years the castle has often been used as a film set.

362-363
Toscana – MONTECARLO | The town of Montecarlo stands on the Cerruglio hill, overlooking the Nievole Valley on one side and the Lucca Plain on the other. Its historic district is dominated by a fortress (left), perched on the top of the hill.

363
Tuscany – FIESOLE | The municipal area of Fiesole, near Florence, has 15,000 inhabitants, a third of whom live in the old town, another third in the Mugnone Valley and the rest in the hamlets, villages and splendid villas (like the one in the photograph) of the Arno Valley.

364-365
Tuscany – MONTEPULCIANO

Montepulciano was founded atop a tuff hill in the 6th century AD and is now a delightful town with an elegant Renaissance appearance. Its heart is Piazza Grande (center), overlooked by the Gothic Town Hall, which resembles the Palazzo Vecchio in Florence.

365
Umbria – GUBBIO

The nickname "City of Silence" seems entirely appropriate for Gubbio, founded at the entrance to a narrow gorge on the slopes of Monte Igino. Its magnificent and entirely medieval historic district is dominated by the Palazzo dei Consoli (center) that forms the boundary of Piazza della Signoria.

366-367
Tuscany – MONTERIGGIONI

Monteriggioni is one of the most famous Italian walled towns. Its walls are interspersed with 14 tower and two gates and surround the old town. Monteriggioni was founded by the Sienese in 1213-1219 on a small hill to control the Elsa and Staggia valleys in the direction of Florence, Siena's historical rival..

368
Lazio - ORTE
The historic district of Orte, in the province of Viterbo, has an unusual teardrop-shaped plan, adapted to the form of the tuff hill on which it stands. The town's strategic position has made it the site of human settlement since ancient times and its history can be traced back as far as the Paleolithic period.

369
Umbria - RIPA
The unusual circular plan of the village of Ripa, near Assisi, is derived from the castle built in 1266 by order of the free commune of Perugia. The purpose of the fortification, whose outer walls had a diameter of over 985 feet, was to keep watch over the boundary with the territory of Assisi and monitor the royal road of Porta Sole leading to Perugia.

370-371
Umbria – SPOLETO
Spoleto, in the heart of Umbria, was home to an important Lombard duchy between the 6th and 8th centuries, and boasts narrow old streets, medieval houses and picturesque squares. Its most important monument is the Cathedral, consecrated in 1198 and preceded by a majestic flight of steps.

372-373 and 373 top
Umbria – ASSISI Assisi, home of Saint Francis, is situated on the slopes of Mount Subasio. The city culminates in the Basilica of St. Francis (large photograph, left), which is formed by two 13th-century churches built one above the other. Its historic district offers many interesting views, including the Piazza del Comune (small photograph).

373 center and bottom
Umbria – ORVIETO Orvieto, of Etruscan origin, is pervaded by a medieval atmosphere that is very evident in Piazza del Popolo (center) and around the 14th-century Cathedral (bottom).

374-375
Umbria - SPELLO The town of Spello is also situated on the slopes of Mount Subasio. It was founded by the Umbrians, played a leading role in the war between Octavian and Mark Antony and witnessed the preaching of Saint Francis. Vineyards and olive groves cover the highly fertile surrounding land.

376-377 | A road through the vineyards leads to the town of Giglio Castello, on the island of Giglio, which has preserved its old
Tuscany – GIGLIO CASTELLO | appearance, enclosed by a ring of medieval walls.

378-379
Tuscany – PORTOFERRAIO | Portoferraio, the capital of Elba, is situated on a rocky spur. Its origins are often associated with the mythical landing of the Argonauts, led by Jason in the quest for the Golden Fleece.

380-381
Lazio – VENTOTENE | Ventotene is the smallest inhabited island of the Pontine Archipelago. Its capital mirrors its extraordinary morphology (it is a tuff island with very steep coasts) of sudden open spaces and small squares, which make it an enchantingly beautiful town.

382-383
Campania – PROCIDA

Procida is situated at the entrance to the Bay of Naples. This island, long a trade hub for great monarchies, has witnessed moments of glory, as testified by the remains of the Castello d'Avalos and the walls that surround the village of Terra Murata, which overlooks Corricella.

383
Campania – ISCHIA

Ischia has always been a strategic trading port. The Aragonese Castle stands on an islet connected to the island by a bridge, symbolizing the age in which Ischia was under Spanish rule.

384-385 and 385
Campania – SORRENTO

Sorrento, situated on evocative rocky bastions, has long enjoyed popularity among high society and lovers of nature and local produce. The numerous little harbors testify to the interest of tourists in rediscovering the coves and small inlets on this stretch of coast, immersed in the fragrance of flowers and citrus groves.

386-387
Apulia – TERLIZZI

Terlizzi Cathedral is the focus of the town and was built over the course of a century, commencing in 1783, on the foundations of the old Romanesque cathedral.

386
Apulia – TERLIZZI

Many of Apulia's small towns are home to authentic artistic and historical masterpieces: left to right, Giovinazzo Cathedral with its two campanili, one Gothic and the other 17th century; Romanesque Trani Cathedral, dedicated to Saint Nicholas Peregrinus, the "queen of Apulia's cathedrals"; the old part of the town of Peschici, on the Gargano Peninsula.

388-389
Apulia – ALBEROBELLO | Alberobello is synonymous with *trulli*, the typical dry-stone houses with large conical roofs, covered with stone shingles known as *chiancole*, which usually rest upon a cubic structure.

390-391
Apulia – GALLIPOLI | The historic district of the town of Gallipoli, on the Ionian Sea, stands on an island connected to the mainland by a bridge. It is surrounded by 16th-century walls that have subsequently been remodeled, even allowing a scenic road to run around the modern town.

392 | Tropea is perched high on a cliff
Calabria – TROPEA | above the waves and was impregnable. The castle that once stood on the site currently occupied by Palazzo Toraldo controlled the only access to the town. These natural bastions are now "balconies" commanding splendid panoramic views.

393 | Rocca Imperiale takes its name from the castle built by Frederick II of Swabia in 1225. The town
Calabria – ROCCA IMPERIALE | extends over the eastern part of the slope and has preserved all its medieval charm, partly because its position makes expansion impossible.

394-395 | This view of Pisticci, in the province of Matera, shows its famous *casedde*: single-story white houses with pointed
Basilicata – PISTICCI | façades arranged in regular terraces sloping from the top to the bottom of the town, which were built to stabilize the slopes. This district was built in 1688 following a great landslide.

**398 top and center
Sicily – EGADI ISLANDS** | The Egadi Islands, west of Sicily, are famous for tuna fishing, which takes place in the ancient *tonnare*. Favignana (left) and Marettimo (right), the capitals of the islands of the same name that are two "floating pearls" set in the Sicilian Sea.

398 bottom and 398-399 Sicily – PELAGIE ISLANDS | The Pelagie Archipelago is situated in the Strait of Sicily, between the island and the coast of Tunisia. Its name is derived from the Greek word *pélagos*, meaning "sea". Lampedusa (bottom), Linosa (right) and uninhabited Lampione are nothing more than enormous volcanic rocks that rose from the seabed. The name of the largest, Lampedusa, is derived from the Byzantine Greek word *Lopadusa*, meaning "rich in mollusks", and refers to the area's plentiful fishing, which has given rise to an excellent cuisine based on seafood and featuring various typical recipes.

400-401
Sardinia – BOSA | Bosa, in the province of Nuoro, on Sardinia's western coast, has developed with a downward movement from the Malaspina Castle to the banks of the Temo River.

400
Sardinia – CARLOFORTE | The port of Carloforte, the only inhabited town on the island of San Pietro, was once used to transport ore from the Sulcis mines, although today its livelihood comes from fishing and tourism.

402-403
Sardinia – ALGHERO | Alghero's historic center has retained its layout of an old maritime town, protected towards the sea by bastions that date back to the construction of a fortified landing place in 1102 by the Doria family of Genoa. The town came under Spanish influence in the 14th century, initially Catalan and Aragonese, followed by the dominant Castilian. This marked the start of a long period of prosperity for the town and considerable expansion in trade.

JOURNEY IN TIME

Modern Italy is dotted with the remains of its ancient

counterpart, which do not coexist easily with the

frenetic pace of consumer culture.

However, the archaeological pearls of the peninsula

gleam for those who wish to see them from the sky,

accompanied only by the rustle of the wind.

JOURNEY IN TIME

ANCIENT ITALY

405
Sicily – TAORMINA

The Theater of Taormina has a Greek plan, but was rebuilt during Roman times (2nd century AD). It is the second largest in Sicily, following that of Syracuse. The *scaena*, featuring three imposing doors, is built of brick and embellished with Corinthian columns. The orchestra, in the center, separates it from the *cavea*, which is divided into nine sectors.

A journey through space and time: our four-dimensional itinerary across the remains of ancient Italy scattered over the modern country allows a clear and complete picture – such as only aerial views can provide – of the passage of the centuries, the traces left on the territory and the very course of Italian civilization. The ways of archaeology are notoriously dusty and often run beneath the ground. However, we offer a bird's-eye view of the past. The land of the prehistoric cultures, Celts, Etruscans, Greeks and above all Romans, has actually been inhabited by a hundred populations, who have left indelible traces within narrow spheres, but whose migrations and assimilations have created civilizations whose influences can still be witnessed throughout the country. The magic of a return to prehistoric times can be experienced by flying over the oldest megalithic sites, from the Valle d'Aosta to Apulia, and onwards as far as the famous and evocative Sardinian *nuraghi* (circular "giants' tombs"). Flying like a bird, it is possible to trace the development of the intricate trading networks of the Copper and Bronze Ages, following the metal, amber and salt routes. Research at the leading archaeological sites has made great progress in uncovering the most significant historical traces of the great process that led to the delineation of the fundamental characteristics of the Italic peoples, from the Celts and the Ligurians to the Samnites and Sardinians, each of which have left indelible signs on a portion of the territory. The trading zeal of the Phoenicians can still be glimpsed at ports such as Motya and Solunto. However, it is necessary to fly to the coasts of the islands and southern Italy to admire the first settlements founded by ancient Greek colonists. The temples of Metapontum, Agrigento, Taormina,

The *Praedia* of Julia Felix and the House of Venus Marina, famous for the fresco from which it takes its name, are situated in *Regio II*, a very built-up district of Pompeii. The Great Theater (visible at the bottom of the photograph on pp. 410-411) announces *Regio VIII*, from which the view of the mysterious and unfortunate Roman city appears to fall away towards Vesuvius.

Syracuse, Selinus and Segesta reveal the creative skill and extraordinary architectural harmony that pervaded the art of Magna Graecia. The Sicilian skies part to make way for dreamlike visions: like Icarus, the reader will float between the clouds that race above the Valley of the Temples, fly over the orange groves and the fascinating Doric buildings erected in ancient Acragas 25 centuries ago and glide above the massive temple at Segesta, before drifting toward the coast, between the pediments and columns of Selinus and over the magical stone segments of the theaters of Taormina and Syracuse. Ancient Greek and Middle Eastern art entered the cultural heritage of the peoples of ancient Italy, becoming part of the Etruscan essence. In some cases they fused and overlapped, as was the case at Paestum, where three Doric temples stand side by side with the Roman forum. When the power and productiveness of Rome, whose architectural expressions were infused with the language of the Greeks, merged with the pragmatism of the Italics, the result was monuments and cities that still constitute essential elements of the panorama of entire regions. The capital itself is a dreamy blend of past and present. Far from the noise of traffic, flying through the capricious sky above the city, ancient Rome appears as a catalogue of treasures: the stone oval of the Colosseum, the network of civic buildings and temples scattered across the grassy expanses of the Imperial Forums, the imposing severity of the Arch of Constantine, the perfect circles formed by the Pantheon and the Mausoleum of Augustus and the grassy oval basin of the Circus Maximus. It is an enormous archaeological garden, in or around which a modern metropolis appears to have casually developed, successfully confining itself and leaving extensive areas of greenery that open like windows onto the city of 2,000 years ago. Traces of Roman civilization are scattered all over the peninsula and Italy was swept by a great wave of art, leaving signs that we can now interpret from our privileged aerial vantage point: from Aosta, Sirmione, Verona and Aquileia to Capri, Pozzuoli, Herculaneum, Oplontis, Paestum and Piazza Armerina. But above all great and unfortunate Pompeii, a gem that the blind cruelty of fate has paradoxically conserved almost intact over the centuries. It is even possible to imagine that time has not passed from above – the distant silhouette of Vesuvius slumbers, while the commercial and residential districts, *decumanus*, forum, great theater and patrician villas seem magically untouched and the city plan intact, in a park where time stands still and the sand of the hourglass ceased to flow at the moment of the fateful eruption.

412

Lazio — ROME

Trajan's Forum (top) was inaugurated in Rome in AD 112. The Colosseum (center) was built around 30 years earlier, on the site of the artificial lake of Nero's Golden House. The valley of the Colosseum is home to the Arch of Constantine (bottom), featuring tondi from the earlier Arch of Hadrian.

412-413 | Varied and confused traces of glory still echo among the ruins scattered across the huge Imperial Forums, in the heart of the Eternal City of Rome,
Lazio – ROME | where time stands still. This magnificent view includes some of the most important buildings, with the Colosseum top right and the arches of the
Basilica of Maxentius and the almost intact Temple of Antonius and Faustina visible on the left. The three famous surviving columns of the Temple
of Vespasian can be seen bottom left, while the Temple of Augustus is visible on the right.

414-415 | The Baths of Caracalla, one of the greatest bath complexes of Imperial Rome, situated near the Appian Way,
Lazio – ROME | owe their name to one of the sons of Septimius Severus: Antoninus Bassianus, who was known as Caracalla.

415 | The huge dome of the Pantheon (top) dates back to the reconstruction of the temple during the rule of Hadrian, although the building was
Lazio – ROME | erected by Marcus Agrippa, son-in-low of Augustus. Augustus himself ordered the construction of what would become his mausoleum
(bottom left), on the Campus Martius, in 28 BC, the year before he became emperor. The ancient Circus Maximus (bottom right) is situated
between the Palatine and Aventine.

416-417

Campania – PAESTUM

The so-called Temple of Ceres" at Paestum – which was actually dedicated to Athena – was built at the end of the 6th century BC by Greek colonists from Sibari, in modern-day Ionian Calabria. It is the smallest of Paestum's three temples and features an interesting combination of two orders: Doric for the peristasis and Ionic for the pronaos.

The same Greek colonists who founded this flourishing city of Magna Graecia also built Paestum's two other temples, dedicated to Hera and known as the Basilica and the Temple of Neptune. The top photograph shows the so-called Basilica on the left, while the two temples can be seen from the opposite side in the picture in the middle, with the Basilica on the right. Its peristasis – with 18 columns on the long sides and 9 on the short ones – can be seen in the bottom photograph.

418-419
Sicily – AGRIGENTO

The rays of the warm Sicilian sun play on the surfaces of the Temple of Concord, one of the architectural masterpieces of Magna Graecia. It was built in Doric style during the first half of the 5th century BC by Greek colonists who had settled in the area at the beginning of the previous century.

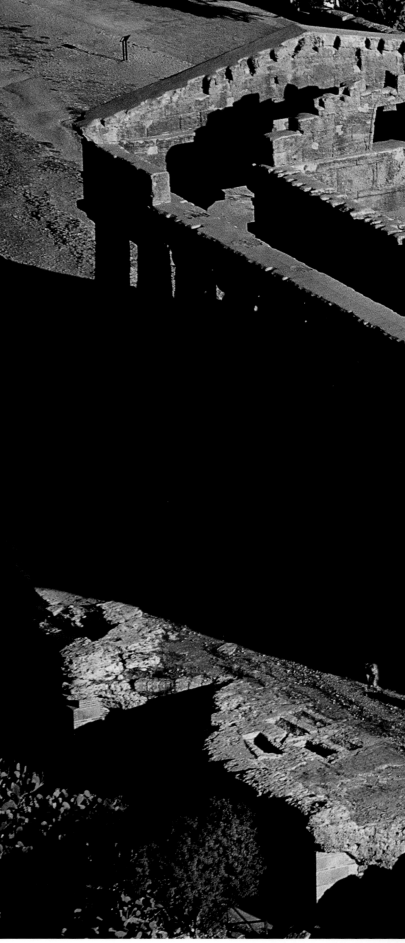

418
Sicily – AGRIGENTO

Only 25 columns remain of the peristasis of the Temple of Hera Lacinia, built around the middle of the 5th century BC in the southern part of the sacred area by the founders of ancient *Acragas* (Greeks from Rhodes and Gela). The wall of the cella is still visible inside.

420-421

Sicily – SYRACUSE

The Greek Theater of Syracuse was inaugurated in the 5th century BC and extended 200 years later. The cavea, measuring 453 feet across, is divided into 9 cunei and is best preserved in the lower part, which is cut into the rock, while the upper section is missing. The classical tradition is revived in this evocative setting in May and June each year, when ancient dramatic works are staged.

421 top

Sicily – SELINUS

Temple E at Selinus was built in Doric style during the first half of the 5th century BC by colonists from Megara Hyblaea, a Greek city on the eastern coast of Sicily. It was dedicated to Hera, the protectress of marriage and fertility, whom the Romans identified with Juno. One of the splendid metopes that once decorated the building depicts the marriage between the goddess and Zeus.

421 bottom

Sicily – SEGESTA

The Greek temple of Segesta (left) can be recognized by its smooth Doric columns, without the usual fluting, and dates back to the second half of the 5th century BC. The theater (right), with its cavea divided into seven cunei, was built later.

422-423
Sicily – TAORMINA | The Greek theater of Taormina assumed its final form during Roman times, in the 2nd century AD. The cavea is surrounded by a wall with ornamental niches; it is still possible to see the complex layout of the structure, with corridors between the stage front and the rooms behind. Today it hosts concerts, theatrical productions and events of various kinds aimed at enhancing the cultural identity of the region.

INDEX

INDEX